LEARN TO FLY AND BECOME A PILOT!

THE ULTIMATE GUIDE FOR DETERMINING YOUR
CAPABILITIES OF BECOMING A PROFESSIONAL
PILOT AND GETTING STARTED WITH FLIGHT
TRAINING

VESA TURPEINEN

PRAISE FOR LEARN TO FLY AND
BECOME A PILOT!

"Having an author with such a wealth of knowledge of flight training, corporate aviation and the aviation industry in China writing about his area of expertise is always hard to come by. Vesa managed to condense a lot of truly useful information in a relatively short and easy to read book which could be the only book you would need for getting started on your aviation career. I followed the same path which Vesa described and it served me well for over 17 years and counting in the aviation industry. I fully recommend this book."

- **Mark Lendvay**, *Airbus A320 Line Training Captain*

"Vesa has done an excellent job at explaining the pros & cons of being a professional pilot. This book also takes you through the various types of pilot jobs out there and there are many...In the book he also lays out how to get qualified and the various paths to this and costs related. Vesa also goes into the available scholarships.

If you are contemplating taking this up as a career this book will help you create a succesful game-plan.

I am an Airline Transport Pilot myself and have flown private jets, air ambulance and for the airlines and I endorse this book!"

- **Fabrizio Poli,** *Aviation Consultant, President of the Beezjet Group, Entrepreneur & ATPL Jet Pilot*

"This book showed me how I could turn my passion for aviation into a career in many areas. It explained in detail the experiences of the author and that not everyone comes from the background you would expect to become a pilot.

Most of all it showed me that anyone can do it! I really liked that it also showed some of the negative aspects and the stress you will encounter, so it is a balanced view of the industry, not just trying to get you to think its always amazing and carefree. Anyone who wants to be a pilot should read this book carefully and then read it again to make sure it sticks.

Overall I think this is a very fair and balanced view of the industry from someone who has lived it for a long time and I consider it a must-read for anyone even thinking of getting into this industry.

- **Jeremy Maswary**, Executive Director of Investment Banking Products

---

"This book does a great job of laying out all the options and paths to a career in aviation. Having the best information on hand helps people make the best decisions possible. I wish I had this book when I was beginning my flight training! It would have made some decisions a lot easier."

- *Preston Seckman*, Falcon 7X / Legacy 650 Corporate Airline Captain

---

"I enjoyed reading Learn To Fly And Become A Pilot! by Vesa Turpeinen and found it a very informative and instructive book, and yet at the same time fun to read. Vesa writes in a casual style without getting too technical about the topic.

Even someone without any flying background can easily follow the subject and it would be especially useful for young students just starting out in school or college to read and understand if this is something that they would truly like to pursue as a career and if so, how to go about it.

This is a great book for anyone interested in the exciting world of flying aircraft and in learning more about that lifestyle."

- **Gisela Dixon,** *Readers' Favorite*

Readers' Favorite®
Book Reviews and Award Contest

2019 INTERNATIONAL BOOK AWARDS
In recognition of excellence in writing

Honorable Mention
Non-Fiction - Education

Learn To Fly And Become A Pilot!
Vesa Turpeinen

Congratulations on your award!
The Readers' Favorite Team

Awards:

Learn to Fly and Become a Pilot! is Readers' Favorite 2019 Honorable Mention Winner (fourth place) in the Non-fiction / Education category.

The Readers' Favorite International Book Award Contest featured thousands of contestants from over a dozen countries, ranging from new independent authors to NYT best-sellers and celebrities. Readers' Favorite is one of the largest book review and award contest sites on the Internet.

They have earned the respect of renowned publishers like Random House, Simon & Schuster, and Harper Collins, and have received the "Best Websites for Authors" and "Honoring Excellence" awards from the Association of Independent Authors. They are also fully accredited by the BBB (A+ rating), which is a rarity among Book Review and Book Award Contest companies.

For my lovely wife Wang Yan.

A SPECIAL FREE GIFT FOR YOU!

As a THANK YOU for purchasing my book, I would like to give you FREE instant access to some bonus materials. The bonus materials include the following:

- Professional Pilot's Guide for Better Sleep and Jet Lag Recovery - 12 Proven Methods to Improve the Quality of Your Sleep

- List of Aviation Scholarships Applicable for Funding Your Flight Training
- List of Questions to Ask When Choosing a Flight School
- Personality of a Pilot - Research Paper

Details at the end of the book. Also, claim your 20% OFF FunkyPilot Store coupon at the end of the book. Most FunkyPilot Store profits go to a flight training scholarship fund that may benefit you or other aspiring pilots in need of financial help. Enjoy the flight!

www.funkypilotstore.com

Copyright and Disclaimer

ISBN 978-952-69238-0-2 Paperback
ISBN 978-952-69238-1-9 Mobi

CONTENTS

INTRODUCTION

"When once you have tasted flight, you will forever walk the earth with your eyes turned skyward, for there you have been, and there you will always long to return."

— Leonardo da Vinci

This quote from Leonardo da Vinci rings very true to most pilots. Once you learn to fly, you're likely to be hooked on aviation for life.

Many people dream of becoming a pilot, but either don't know how to get started or don't believe they have the necessary skills. But here's some good news: if you're reading this book, you can probably become a pilot! And guess what? You could become a professional pilot, or even a flight instructor, with less than a year of training!

Becoming a pilot isn't as difficult as you might think. Of course, it takes a lot of hard work and dedication, but it's a logical, step-by-step process that builds upon previously-learned skills and knowledge.

You don't need to be unusually intelligent to be a pilot. If you're capable of learning to drive a car, you are probably capable of learning to fly a plane. Actually, you don't even need to know how to drive a car to become a pilot!

The medical requirements for pilots are also not as strict as you might think. There are commercial pilots who are deaf, armless, or who have other disabilities. Some limitations apply to those pilots of course, and they may not be able to work in passenger transportation. But they can still work as commercial pilots for other types of flying.

It's important to remember that you don't have to work for a commercial airline to enjoy a career as a pilot. Although most people who are training to become pilots aim for commercial airline jobs, there's a lot more to being a pilot than transporting passengers from one place to another. There are many different types of pilot jobs; you just need to choose the path that fits you the best.

The biggest obstacle for most people dreaming of life as a pilot is the financial investment necessary to get started. However, while flight training is expensive, you don't need to be a multi-millionaire to get started. A portion of this book is dedicated to highlighting several methods you might be able to use to finance your training. It might surprise you to learn that there are many scholarships, student loans, and other types of financial aid available for hopeful pilots.

Additionally, some people are under the assumption that an expensive college degree is necessary in order to pursue a career in aviation. While having a college degree will certainly help you later in your career, you don't need one to get started with your flight training. You can start your flight training straight out of high school (or even before that). And investing your money in flight training, which leads to an exciting and possibly well-paying career, might be money more wisely spent than on a degree you may or may not need.

Another thing I want to mention in this introduction is that **RIGHT NOW** is an excellent time to get started with a pilot career! And I will tell you why.

In 2019 there was a global shortage of pilots predicted to last for at least the next two decades. The COVID-19 pandemic changed things quite a bit; thousands of pilots got furloughed, and it created a significant oversupply of qualified pilots in the job market. The surplus of pilots, however, is temporary. Many of the furloughed pilots are facing a mandatory retirement age in the near future. Other pilots may have found employment doing something else. They may not want to come back to flying even when there is an opportunity for it.

In 2020 many flight schools trained fewer pilots than usual because many aspiring pilots either delayed their training or completely changed their career plans.

While the airlines experienced significant losses due to the COVID-19, the private jet sector is making record sales – more and more wealthy people are purchasing private jets to avoid airline crowds. This has created a need for more pilots in the private sector.

And as time passes, more and more COVID vaccinations are being introduced, and people are eager to travel again. It is expected that air travel will return to 2019 levels within the next couple of years and then will continue to increase as predicted earlier.

While the pandemic has undoubtedly had a devastating effect on the airline industry, you shouldn't give up on your dreams of becoming a pilot because of it – in the long term, pilots are still needed. When things start picking up again, there may not be enough pilots returning to work, which makes this a good time for you to begin your flight training to become a pilot.

If you start now, you could be working as a commercial pilot within a year. That means a pilot career might still be a good option for people in their 30s, 40s or even 50s!

Of course, it's better to get started at an early age if you can. You can get a student pilot certificate at the age of 16, a private pilot certificate at the age of 17, and start flying as a commercial pilot when you are only 18 years old! Any parents reading this may want to keep that in mind for their children.

If you're about to graduate from high school and are looking for an exciting and profitable career, keep reading. Or if you're looking for a career transition that will give you the opportunity to spend your life doing something more fun and rewarding than your current nine-to-five, you should also keep reading.

Whatever your situation and motivation for reading this book might be, my hope is that it will be a valuable resource and a first step on your journey to becoming a professional pilot!

ABOUT THIS BOOK

This book will explain the steps you need to take to determine whether you can become a pilot. It will also describe the things you need to consider before committing your time and money to flight training, and will show you how to get started if a career as a pilot sounds right for you.

This book is for you if any of the following apply:

- You have always dreamed of becoming a pilot, but don't know how to get started

- You want to be a pilot, but don't know if it's possible or realistic

- You have a child and are wondering if a career as a pilot is a good option for him/her

- You want a career that gives you the chance to travel and see the world

- You want a career that's exciting, fun and rewarding

This book is primarily intended for people seeking a career as a professional pilot, but it's a useful read even if you're just interested in attaining a private pilot license so you can fly for fun.

It's not within the scope of the book to cover different aviation knowledge subjects in detail, but I will provide links to many free manuals that you can use later on during your flight training.

The information in this book mostly applies to flight training in the United States, following the regulations set by the Federal Aviation Administration (FAA). However, you can still benefit from reading this book even if you're planning to do your training in another country.

I purposefully wrote the book in a casual tone. Many aviation books are full of regulations and technical details that can be super boring (you'll see what I mean when you actually start studying some of the FAA handbooks). That's a shame, because flying is incredibly fun and exciting! I want you to enjoy reading this book, to feel excited about beginning your journey to become a pilot, and to have enough information to get started down that path. You don't need to know all the regulations and rules now—you'll have plenty of time to learn them later. (And trust me, you can.)

I also made this book short and easy to read on a Kindle or other e-reader. I hope you'll be able to finish it before you get bored and give up on pursuing your dream of becoming a pilot!

Throughout the book there are little endnote marks such as this: [1]. The endnotes indicate links to different resources. You can find all the links at the end of the book from the "notes". For your convenience, I have also compiled all the links in one location on my resources page at https://www.funkypilot.com/resources[2], so you can easily visit them after you have finished the book.

A BRIEF STORY ABOUT MY LIFE IN AVIATION

Y ou may be wondering who I am and what qualifies me to write about aviation. Everyone has their own story about how they got started in their particular field of expertise. I am only one pilot among thousands, but understanding where I come from and how I got started as a pilot may show you that your dreams of flight are within reach.

Here is my story.

GROWING UP IN FINLAND

Growing up in Finland, I had nothing to do with aviation. Well, I may have parachuted from an airplane a few times, but jumping out of a perfectly good aircraft is frowned upon by many pilots. Anyway, I had nothing to do with aviation until after graduating from high school.

I graduated from high school in Helsinki in 1998, and around that time my older brother started a flight training program in Conway, South Carolina. And in 1999 while I was struggling through my military training, which is mandatory for all young men in Finland, he was already working as a flight instructor in New Jersey. Wait! He started flight training in 1998, and one year later was already teaching other people how to fly?! Yes. Becoming a professional pilot, and even a flight instructor, can be accomplished that quickly!

I did those parachute jumps I mentioned earlier while in the military, by the way. At the time, I was mostly interested in physical fitness and had no intention of becoming a pilot. I didn't even think I could ever be capable of flying a plane. After all, I wasn't even comfortable with the stick-shift in my dad's car.

Interest in Aviation Sparked

After many phone conversations with my brother, after reading emails where he talked about the exhilaration of flying, and after seeing pictures from his flight school, things changed. It all sparked my interest in becoming a pilot myself.

I had been admitted to study mechanical engineering in Helsinki. In fact, I briefly studied it, between my high-school graduation and the start of my military training. But I had to put it on hold. My studies were supposed to start again after my military training. This would have been a free education from one of the top schools in Finland. But I decided to call it quits.

Flying a plane seemed far more fun and interesting to me than studying engineering. I was also very excited about visiting the United States, thanks to all the American TV shows and Hollywood movies I had seen while growing up!

At the time, the flight school in Conway was recruiting students from Finland, Sweden, Norway, and other northern European countries. It was running newspaper ads in Helsinki, and held recruitment events in the city for potential flight training candidates. I contacted the school, and I was asked to attend an admission test held in a rented conference room downtown.

Flight School Admission Test

I had to complete a pilot aptitude test that included some basic math and problem solving, as well as an English test. It was all fairly easy, and I was well-prepared thanks to my brother's help. The most difficult part for me was speaking in English to the flight school managers during a short interview. Finnish is my native language, and although I had studied English in school, I didn't have much practical experience speaking it at the time.

I did OK though, and passed the admission test. It felt great! I took that test in late 1999, and my flight training was supposed to start a few months later. It gave me some time to get all my visa papers and financial arrangements in order. These were exciting times!

Why the Testing?

You might be aware that pilots usually pay for their own training. So why the testing? The purpose of the admission test was to select candidates who were likely to complete the professional pilot training program offered by the school.

Of course, the training was still paid for by the students—but the school was responsible for maintaining certain student standards, and the pre-admission screening process helped with that. If the school had admitted all paying applicants, it might have caused problems when some students couldn't keep up with the training and had to drop out.

Students pay for the training in installments, so

when a student drops out the school loses the remaining payments and has to find new students in order to continue generating revenue. Also, the school would be in danger of losing its flight school certificate if too many students failed the official FAA examinations.

Admission tests are a fairly common practice for bigger flight schools, but not for smaller ones. These types of tests are also more common in Europe than in the United States.

SEVEN YEARS IN THE UNITED STATES

I started my flight training in March of 2000, in Conway, South Carolina. The school was called the North American Institute of Aviation (or NAIA for short). It took me just over a year to complete the school's professional pilot training program.

The program provided full training: from being a complete beginner who had never been in even a small plane, to becoming a commercial pilot with single-engine and multi-engine instrument airplane endorsements. In addition to the commercial pilot training, I also trained to be a certified flight and ground instructor while I was there.

My visa was valid for only two years, so I was eager to find a job as a flight instructor soon after graduation. After completing the pilot training program, I moved to Florida to work at a flight school. There, I gained more experience flying different types of airplanes and teaching students from different nationalities.

By the time my visa expired, I had accrued about 1,000 hours of flight experience—most of it as a flight instructor. I liked what I was doing, and I enjoyed living in Florida, so I was determined to find a way to extend my stay in the United States.

Studies at Embry-Ridde Aeronautical University

Instead of packing my bags and heading back to Finland, I applied to study at Embry-Riddle Aeronautical University, which is the largest and most widely-recognized aeronautical university in the world. Conveniently, the school had a campus in Orlando, where I was living at the time.

I was accepted, and I began my studies in May of 2002. Enrolling at Embry-Riddle renewed my visa, which allowed me to stay in the country. The renewal was for four years of study, plus a six-month period for paid professional training. I completed my bachelor's degree in professional aeronautics in just over two years, and after graduation I went to work in the field of aviation, where I planned to spend the next six months.

So what kind of job did I decide to do? Well, I went back to flight instructing. I flew the crap out of some small Cessnas during that period. Seven days per week, eight flight hours per day whenever possible, for about four months straight. After that, believe it or not, I decided to go back to school again.

I had to figure out what to do after my six-month work training period ended. Although my visa was valid for nearly two more years, it was useless since I had graduated and I could only work for a limited time. So I decided to study some more.

I liked studying at Embry-Riddle. And although I loved flying, I was also interested in starting my own business someday. So why not study business? Embry-Riddle offered a master's degree in business administration (MBA) specifically focused on the aviation industry. It sounded like a perfect program for me, so I applied.

During the few months I was teaching students to fly, I also had to study for either the Graduate Management Admission Test (GMAT). It was a pain to study and work at the same time, but I got it done. I started my MBA program in January of 2005 and finished about a year and a half later.

Internship at DFW Airport

As part of my MBA studies, I got an internship at the Dallas/Fort Worth International Airport (DFW) in 2006. My three-month internship turned into eight months, and I was looking at a permanent airport job. Unfortunately, the airport, as a government company, could not help me get a work visa or a green card. My latest student visa again allowed me to work in aviation-related companies, but the visa expiration was approaching.

No more studying, I decided. I had an astronomical amount of student loans to pay back (in the six figures), and I had stayed in the United States for nearly seven years with barely any income; the few months that I worked as a flight instructor or as an intern had covered only my living expenses at the time, nothing else—no savings, no paying back loans.

I applied to a few jobs with private companies and airlines that would have made use of my MBA, without much luck. But I also had to be honest with myself; I wasn't really enjoying office work. I missed flying.

Although I hadn't been flying much during my MBA studies, I started looking for pilot jobs again. I did enjoy working at DFW Airport, but the office work in such a big organization seemed meaningless and was quite boring. I wanted to get back in the air and feel the excitement of flying again. I was a pilot, after all.

The only problem was that it was even more difficult to find companies that could sponsor foreigners for pilot jobs than for MBA-related jobs. Every single pilot job opening had this requirement: U.S. citizen. So I decided it was time for a change of scenery.

What to do next?

Going back to Finland didn't seem too appealing. My degrees from the United States wouldn't do me much good in my home country, and I couldn't fly there with my FAA licenses. The long and expensive process of converting my pilot licenses to European ones didn't interest me at all. That would have meant taking more loans and moving back in to live with my parents. No thanks! I needed a paying job.

A DECADE IN CHINA AND COUNTING

I discovered that there was a huge demand for pilots across Asia, and especially in China. In fact, I found a Chinese flight school that was looking for foreign instructors.

It was the first privately owned flight school in the country, and they wanted English-speaking instructors so the students would learn English while they learned to fly. English is the international language of aviation (*lingua franca*), which is why most flight schools around the world operate in English.

The pay was good, too. The guaranteed monthly salary was more than twice what I had earned as a flight instructor in Florida, and the cost of living was substantially lower—especially considering that housing and daily transportation to and from the airport was included.

Moving to China

I moved to China in March of 2007, and it has been one of the best decisions I have ever made. Converting my FAA pilot licenses to Chinese ones was easy. The school had instructors from over a dozen countries, 60 airplanes, and hundreds of students contracted by several different Chinese airlines.

I started as a regular flight instructor. After a few months, I was promoted to the position of check instructor, which meant that I performed progress checks on other instructors' students.

And during my second year in China, I was promoted to the position of assistant chief flight instructor for the school. Essentially, I got to be in charge of all the flight operations on one of the four campuses the flight school operated.

Working as a Chief Flight Instructor

After two years with the private flight school, I was hired to be the chief flight instructor at the second largest government-owned flight school in China.

How cool was that!? There I was, a lone Finnish guy in the most populous country in the world, and they wanted *me* as the chief pilot at one of their most important flight training centers!

It was an extremely rare opportunity that I was lucky to be given. I ended up working as the chief flight instructor at the school for just over three years.

It was a great experience. I was in charge of most of the students' training progress, as well as instructor standards. The job was a perfect mix of office work and flying.

Although the pay for the role of chief flight instructor was good, I had reached the cap after three years on the job. I knew the airlines and corporate aviation jobs in China were paying much better. Also, my initial excitement about the job had died down, and some conflicts with other managers had started to emerge. So, I decided to move on.

I could talk a lot about my experiences as a flight instructor in China, but that's a subject for another book. In fact, I plan to talk more about all my experiences as a flight instructor in the third book of the *Pilot Career* series.

Job as a Corporate Pilot

In 2012, I started working for a Chinese corporate jet management company. Since then, I have flown Bombardier Challenger 605s and 650s. The Challenger is a medium-range, medium-size business jet manufactured in Canada.

Taking a job as a first officer initially felt like a demotion. I had spent the last four years being in charge of things, after all—first as an assistant chief flight instructor, and then as a chief flight instructor at school with over 60 airplanes. Working as a first officer on a three-person crew (two pilots and one flight attendant) was quite a change.

But today I have no regrets. Flying a corporate jet has proven to be a better job than I ever imagined. It has been a great experience to fly a pressurized aircraft at high altitudes at close to the speed of sound.

Instead of just buzzing around with those tiny flight training planes, over the last few years I've had the opportunity to visit five continents, dozens of countries, and countless cities—all while flying amazing and incredibly expensive aircraft.

Now I work as a captain, and that means that if anything goes wrong it's my fault. And when you operate such a complex aircraft and carry passengers at high altitudes, a lot of things can go wrong. But I find these responsibilities less stressful than working in a management position and being in charge of multiple things as opposed to just one aircraft. And another great thing about corporate flying is that I don't have to bring my job home after a flight.

During my free time, I don't need to think too much about work—other than what to pack for the next trip. This job has given me time to start blogging[1] and writing this book (with more books on the way).

Time to Craft Your Story in Aviation!

I hope you find this book useful and inspiring. I hope it motivates you to follow your dreams of becoming a professional pilot—whether your goal is to be a commercial airline pilot or a corporate captain like me. If you thought it would never be possible for you to become a pilot, perhaps this book will change your mind.

-Vesa Turpeinen

NOTE TO MY INTERNATIONAL READERS:

As I already mentioned, this book focuses on flight training in the United States. And from my story, you know that I ended up in China because I didn't feel like going through the long and expensive process of converting my FAA certificates to European ones.

Ideally, it would be most convenient to train in your home country (or in the country where you plan to work after graduation). That way, you won't have to worry about converting your licenses later on.

For some of you, it might still make sense to train in the United States, or in another country where you can complete the training faster and cheaper than at home. In any case, before you commit to training in a foreign country, please make sure you know what to do after you have your pilot certificates.

The conversion process is usually not that difficult if you prepare for it in advance. And there are actually flight schools that offer programs that include joint training for both the FAA and EASA (European Aviation Safety Agency) certificates.

Choosing a flight school that offers both FAA and EASA certificates would probably be the best option for most European pilot students, because then you will have the benefit of having the FAA certificates for future job opportunities.

No matter what country you're from, it's a good idea to find a school that has experience with international students from your homeland. This means the school will be better prepared to accommodate your needs. More about choosing a flight school is provided later in this book.

Can I fly with FAA certificates in other countries? And why don't you work in Europe?

Most countries follow rules set by the International Civil Aviation Organization (ICAO) and conduct civil flight training in very similar ways. Pilot certificates issued by those countries can, in most cases, be converted to an equivalent license in another ICAO country.

The conversion is done by completing a variety of practical and theory-based exams. Even if you decide to do your training in the United States, you won't have to go through the whole training process again in your home country.

For example, I completed my training in the United States and have all my pilot certificates issued by the FAA. I also have an Airline Transport Pilot License, which is issued by the CAAC (Civil Aviation Administration of China).

With these certificates and licenses, I can fly anywhere in the world in a U.S.-registered or Chinese-registered aircraft. To fly airplanes registered in other countries, I would have to get that country's license (or some other type of validation of my existing licenses).

In my case, as a Finnish citizen, I could easily work just about anywhere in Europe. But in order to fly an aircraft *registered* in Europe, I would need to convert my FAA or CAAC license into an EASA (European Aviation Safety Agency) license.

However, even without the EASA license, I could find a way to work in Europe. For example, there are some airplanes that are based in Europe but which are registered in the United States, and I can fly those with my FAA license.

Also, some airplanes are registered in countries that validate other countries' licenses with some simple paperwork (such as the Isle of Man or the Cayman Islands); I could fly those planes, as well.

Actually, I have flown a Chinese-registered Challenger 605 in many European countries. If that same aircraft was sold to someone in Europe, and the registration was changed, I would not be allowed to fly it.

These are some of the small annoyances you may face in the future if you end up working or training in different countries.

A good thing to keep in mind at this point is that the pilot license you need is not always based on the country where you plan to work. The license you need is based on the registration country of the aircraft you plan to fly.

3

WHY BECOME A PILOT?

The short answer is: why *not* become a pilot? There are many reasons why people want to fly. Most of the pilots I meet say they have always wanted to fly. Becoming a pilot was their dream since they were kids, and they worked hard to make that dream a reality.

Then again, many pilots just end up flying because they follow in the footsteps of their friends or family. That's what happened to me. It wasn't my childhood dream to be a pilot; I just kind of ended up being one because my brother was, and I didn't know what else to do with my life.

Being a pilot can be a very rewarding career path. If you're searching for adventure, excitement, and opportunities to travel, then a career as a pilot could be a great choice for you.

In my previous job as a flight instructor, I had many students in their 50s tell me that they finally had the money to own a small private aircraft, so they wanted to learn to fly. The feeling of freedom you experience while flying solo in a small airplane can be very rewarding.

These are all good reasons to learn how to fly. If you choose to embark on a flight training journey, I doubt you'll regret it. Even if flying hasn't been your dream or aviation isn't your passion, I'm confident it will grow on you once you get started!

In this chapter, you'll learn about the benefits of becoming a pilot and why it might be a good career choice for you.

INDUSTRY OUTLOOK

Based on Boeing's 2020 Pilot Outlook[1], there will be worldwide demand for 763,000 new pilots between 2020 and 2039. The Asia-Pacific region has the highest demand, needing to hire over 248,000 new pilots during that period. Demand for qualified pilots in Asia has already been high for many years, which is why I ended up in China. The next-largest demand will be in the United States (208,000 pilots needed) followed by

Europe (147,000 pilots needed). That's *a lot* of new pilots!

But don't get too excited just yet. Although there was a shortage of pilots already in 2019, there were still many unemployed pilots looking for jobs. Why? Because the airlines need *experienced* pilots with "type ratings" (which are like endorsements on a driver's license) in large passenger aircraft, such as the planes built by Boeing and Airbus.

Low-time pilots straight out of flight schools can still have a hard time finding good jobs to advance their careers. What makes things even more difficult for low-time pilots is that some countries or airlines select their pilot candidates through a rigorous application process and then train them from the ground up. These airlines typically won't even consider other applicants.

But things are constantly changing. According to 2019 news reports, some airlines were already reducing routes or grounding planes because of the pilot shortage. I believe that for them to stay in business after the COVID-19, they need to provide opportunities and train low-time pilots up to the airline's standards, and provide training for aircraft "type ratings" when necessary.

I'm confident that with hard work, research, and

dedication most pilots can find decent jobs. And I'm confident that you'll be able to find one too!

After reading this book, please join my Facebook group[2] at https://facebook.com/groups/pilotcareers to find job opportunities and to discuss any aspects of pilot training and aviation careers.

One more thing I want to mention here: you will probably meet many people who say the pilot shortage is a myth. In fact, someone recently told me the market is "full and overflowing" and that I have read too much "fake advertising." He didn't elaborate on what he meant by "fake advertising."

It's up to you to draw your own conclusions from everything you read, but in China, for example, some airline captains make up to $380,000 per year flying an Airbus 320 or a Boeing 737. I don't think airlines would pay that much (especially to foreigners) if they had an overflow of pilots...

PILOT SALARIES

Does it make financial sense to go through all the trouble and uncertainty of becoming a pilot?

Well, that's a question you have to answer for yourself, based on your own unique circumstances. Still, there are some general things you should think about as you evaluate your options.

People often ask me about my salary. It would be a violation of my contract to discuss my salary, but I can give a basic idea of your potential earnings outlook if you were to decide to follow this career path.

All the salary and expense figures in this book are in U.S. dollars unless otherwise stated.

According to the United States Bureau of Labor Statistics[3], the median annual pay for scheduled airline pilots in May 2017 was $140,530, while for non-scheduled commercial air transportation pilots the median annual pay was $78,610.

Scheduled airline pilots work for regional or major airlines that fly regular routes and follow set schedules that have been planned months (or even years) in advance.

Non-scheduled pilots work for charter airlines, corporate aviation companies, or other aviation companies providing air transportation based on demand.

The lowest 10 percent of commercial pilots earned less than $43,570 annually. These numbers are just a small sample statistic; you can easily find pilot jobs that pay as little as $10 per hour, while some senior airline captains can earn in excess of $300,000 per year.

Thanks to the high demand for pilots, salaries have increased sharply in recent years. Instead of starting with an annual salary of less than $20,000 at regional airlines, you can now find regional airline jobs that offer over $60,000 in the first year.

Salaries have increased in the United States, but you can find even better-paying pilot jobs in Asia. Chinese airlines in particular are constantly looking to hire foreign captains.

Once you have 500 hours or more as a Boeing or Airbus captain, you could find a job with a net salary of $200,000 to $380,000 per year.

Let that sink in for a moment. The lower end of the scale is around $16,000 per month. The higher end of the scale is over $30,000 per month. And that's the net salary after Chinese income taxes!

I'm not trying to rub it in, but think about it: some foreign airline captains in China make around a million dollars in just three years! It's hard work, of course.

The Chinese airlines get their money's worth by making pilots work non-stop within the legal limits of their duty times. And it may be difficult to get into these jobs; the Chinese pilot medical exams are not easy to pass, and moving to another country may not be convenient for pilots with families.

Also, many qualified pilots are reluctant to leave their stable jobs in their home countries for a temporary gig in Asia. If they wanted to return to their old airline after a few years in China, they would have lost all the seniority benefits they had accumulated the first time around.

But the high salaries in China should be motivational for those of you who are in it for the money. For corporate pilots, salaries are usually a bit lower, but still solid.

If you're reading this book, chances are you're not yet a pilot. I'm only mentioning these salaries to keep you motivated about the potential payoffs. Flying small planes is a lot of fun, but when you get to the big ones, it's serious business with serious benefits.

And frankly, I'm mentioning the jobs in China in part because I'm very familiar with flying and living in the country.

———

Those are the well-paying pilot jobs. But to be honest, you shouldn't focus on the pay when you first get started with flying. For the first few years of your pilot career, you will most likely struggle to pay your monthly bills, and you may have to find a roommate (or more likely several of them) to share your living expenses.

Flight instruction, glider towing, and other general aviation jobs usually don't pay much, so keep that in mind. And although you can expect regular pay increases as you advance your career, there are no guarantees that you will ever get one of those extremely high-paying airline captain jobs — only a small number of pilots will ever make in excess of $200K or $300K per year.

For information about pilot salaries and pilot jobs available in China, you can check out my resources page at: https://www.funkypilot.com/resources.

THE EXCITEMENT AND ADVENTURE OF FLYING

"Adventure is worthwhile in itself." — *Amelia Earhart*

Your initial flight training will be one of the most exciting periods of your life. You will learn new skills and gain an overwhelming amount of new knowledge at a rapid pace.

But the adventure continues throughout your career. It's very exciting to fly new types of airplanes, to fly with different pilots, and to fly to different cities, countries and continents.

As a pilot, you may get to fly crop dusters or firefighting planes close to the ground. You may get to visit dozens of countries flying at 50,000 feet in a private jet. Or one day, you might be responsible for landing massive double-decker airliners carrying hundreds of passengers.

Pilots can choose between many exciting career paths that are all worth overcoming the obstacles to achieve. Simply the joy of flying is the best benefit of the career for many pilots. Most pilots I know wouldn't change their careers for anything. They simply enjoy flying too much — no matter whether they fly big or small airplanes.

While flying is hard work at times, it can be a very enjoyable way of living — I know I enjoy it. For many, flying can be hard work that doesn't feel like work. While I do get tired of flying at times, I always turn my head toward the sky when I hear an airplane passing by — and can't wait to get back in the air myself.

Something I Often Think to Myself During a Flight

I often find myself thinking how lucky I'm sitting here at 39,000 feet, at night, over Siberia, heading to Alaska. With our instrument panels dimmed to a minimum, the sky above us is bright with stars, planets, and colorful northern lights, and we can see blinking satellites flying by on the orbit, with Milky Way on the background. It's a sight most people will never experience, and even the best cameras won't make it justice.

I doubt you'll ever get bored with your job if you choose a career in aviation!

TRAVEL, HOTEL, AND FLIGHT BENEFITS

As a career pilot you will end up traveling a lot. The job of an airline pilot is to transport people or cargo from one place to another.

Airline Pilot Benefits

A major benefit of working for airlines is the travel benefits they offer. If you work for an airline, you can usually fly nearly free of charge on any of your company flights when there are empty seats on the plane.

The same goes with other airline flights that have code-share agreements with your airline. If you like to travel a lot during your free time, then these travel benefits can add up to substantial savings each year. These benefits can also usually be extended to your immediate family, so you're likely to gain a lot of family support for your career choice!

Traveling for work can be counted as a benefit in and of itself. Especially on long-distance flights, you will usually get to spend a fair amount of nights in the destinations your airline serves. As a corporate pilot, I usually pack my luggage the same way as I would when going on a vacation.

Corporate Pilot Benefits

Corporate pilots don't have the same travel benefits that are offered to commercial pilots. For example, I don't get any free flights from airlines. But we do have some hotel benefits instead. Because I normally stay in hotels over 100 nights per year, I always try to stay at places that belong to the same chain. That way, I earn substantial amounts of membership points. I can use those points for free nights in hotels during my vacations, or I can even use them for free flights with participating airlines. For more information about the subject, you might want to read my blog post titled "Corporate Pilot's Guide to Hotel Benefits[4]."

Visit Places not Serviced by Airlines

Corporate pilots may also get to travel to places not serviced by airlines. Sometimes you may get to spend several days, or even weeks, in places you didn't even know existed. Of course, destinations that are not served by airlines may not interest many people, but if you are into "authentic" travel experiences, then flying business jets might be a good fit for you.

Traveling for Training

In addition to flight trips, your regular recurrent training may involve traveling to different countries or cities where the simulators are located. Recurrent training usually takes about a week, while initial training for a new "type rating" can take up to a month. I visit Dubai about every six months for my regular recurrent training; there, I review all kinds of emergency procedures for my aircraft type.

While Dubai is my regular place for recurrent training, I also do regular emergency training in the United States. I usually go there every two years for training that involves firefighting in a mock cockpit and jumping into a pool with a life raft. Not only is the training exciting and important, but I can usually connect these trips with my personal vacation days to get more out of them.

TIME OFF

Don't get too excited about having much time off early in your career. You will most likely be working seven days per week for the first couple of years. You won't have the time or money to take vacations. You'll just be focusing on gaining flight experience and working as much as you can.

Luckily, once you get a decent airline or corporate pilot job, things will be different. With the airlines, you're very likely to be guaranteed at least eight days off per month. And with seniority, you'll have even more.

With corporate pilot jobs you will probably be on standby a lot, but you will do this at home while collecting salary. If you choose to work internationally in Asia or in the Middle East, you could even get a rotational job. With these jobs, you work for some set period (30 days straight, for example) and then take a similar set period off. In that scenario, you would only work for about six months out of the year while still earning a good salary!

.   .   .

Not many professional careers offer so much flexibility.

OTHER BENEFITS

There are countless other benefits associated with becoming a pilot. Of course, every pilot considers different things "benefits." For example, there's a certain coolness or prestige factor that comes with being a pilot. You should watch the film *Catch me if You Can*[5] to see what I mean. Of course, that's a story about a criminal, but it still gives a glimpse of the respect people often show to pilots.

When I tell people what I do for a living, many people say things like, "Ooohh, you're a Pilot? So exciting!" That's certainly not a benefit in the technical sense, but it can be fun—and it's often a great icebreaker that allows me to meet new and interesting people.

One thing I personally think is a valuable benefit is the "exciting career" factor. Pilots get to operate some very expensive high-tech equipment. Every time I get to fly new types of airplanes, I consider it a privilege. I find it interesting and rewarding to fly new planes, and sometimes it's still hard to believe I get paid to do it.

FIND YOUR WHY

Before you commit to flight training, you should find your "why." Why do you want to be a pilot? Do you want to do it for the excitement and adventure? For the money and prestige? To travel and see the world?

You should also think about your long-term aviation goals. Do you want to become a career pilot, or just get a private license? And if your answer is the latter, what do you intend to do with it? Answering questions like these will help you choose the right flight school.

Think about it. No matter what your "why" is, you need to make sure it outweighs the downsides of a flight career. Because just like with any career, there *are* many downsides. But if you have a clear goal in mind and a passion for aviation, it will be easier to stay motivated to go through all the headaches of pilot training.

Just one word of warning, though — if you want to be a pilot because you are looking for money or status, you may end up disappointed and struggle with your career. Flying is a career that requires real dedication and hard work to be successful.

Chapter 1 Key Takeaways

- It's hard to deny that the job market looks good for pilots. But keep in mind, it's a very dynamic industry that is constantly changing.

- Pilot salaries vary significantly from job to job and from country to country. In general the salaries are better in Asia, but there has been some improvement in salaries across the board. You can expect to make a decent living—and potentially even a great living—as a career pilot. But money shouldn't be your only motivation for pursuing this career.

- The excitement and adventure of flying can, in and of itself, be the main reward for choosing to become a pilot.

- If you love to travel, commercial airline and corporate pilots can enjoy many benefits—like free flights and great hotel deals—that can make aviation a worthwhile career choice.

- You won't have much time off in the early days of your career. But depending on the job, you can expect a lot of free time later on.

- You should spend some time thinking about why you want to become a pilot. Any reason is as good as any other, but having a clear idea about why you want to pursue this goal will help you stay motivated when the path is challenging.

In this chapter, I talked about the benefits of a flight career and why people choose to become pilots. In the next chapter, I'll talk about the potential downsides of that choice.

THE DOWNSIDES OF A CAREER IN AVIATION

Before you commit to becoming a professional pilot, you should be aware that there are some serious downsides to this particular career. Even if it's your dream, you need to understand that working as a pilot is definitely not suitable for everyone.

This chapter will cover the major downsides of a career in aviation so that you can better determine whether it's the right choice for you.

EXPENSIVE TO GET STARTED

There is an old saying about aviation: "If you want to make a small fortune in aviation, start with a big one!"

Becoming a pilot can be very expensive. Flight training is not cheap, so unless you already have a decent amount of savings, you will almost certainly have to borrow money from banks, relatives, or some other source.

Or you might have to work one or several jobs while training, which will make the program longer and more difficult than necessary. I financed my training through several bank loans and help from my father.

Loans can take a long time to pay back, and you may even have a hard time getting one that will cover all your flight training expenses.

Although flight training is expensive, don't give up on your dream of becoming a pilot because of the initial costs!

Keep on reading—in Chapter 6, I will explain several methods you can use to finance your training. You might be surprised to learn about all the different options that are available to you.

TIME AWAY FROM HOME

If your goal is to become an airline pilot or a corporate aviation pilot, you will end up traveling a lot. And that means you will spend many nights away from home.

While it's fun and exciting to travel around the world (especially while getting paid to do so), it can take a toll on your relationships and family life.

There is a relatively high divorce rate among pilots because it can be difficult to maintain a relationship when you spend most of your time on the road—or in the air, to be more specific.

You Are Likely to Miss Important Events

As a pilot, you're likely to miss many important events like birthday parties, anniversaries, your friends' weddings, family gatherings and holidays.

This is definitely something to discuss with your spouse before starting an airline or corporate pilot career. Even if you both think you are prepared for it, you probably aren't.

Don't be surprised by the stress and arguments that arise when you actually start missing important events!

Even after flying for many years, it didn't go that well when I missed Valentine's Day 2019; instead of spending the day with my wife, I was in some hotel room in Hong Kong. Oh, well... at least I got to work on this book!

Of course, if you're single then you're in a better position to handle difficult flight schedules. But keep in mind that it will be tough to start any serious relationships if you're constantly traveling.

. . .

The good news is that there are many different types of pilot career options that won't involve quite so much traveling. I will discuss different career paths in Chapter 3.

Also, it's good to keep in mind that many pilots who discuss the positive and negative sides of their career with their spouses do manage to have good family lives. Honesty about the job and how it will affect family life goes a long way to having a well-balanced work and family life.

LOW-PAYING PILOT JOBS

Not all pilot jobs pay that well. When I started working as a flight instructor, I was getting paid about $10 per flight hour. In a busy month, I would fly around 100 hours if I had enough students (and if I worked seven days per week).

That was a lot of work for just $1,000 in pay. After taxes and living expenses, I rarely had any money left. I was living from paycheck to paycheck. I couldn't even think about starting to pay back my loans with that kind of income.

All of my colleagues had the same struggles; I know, because I used to be roommates with many of them. None of us could afford to live alone.

This was in 2001 and 2002, working for a decent size flight school in Florida. I'm sure there are much better-paying flight schools to work for, but when you're looking for your first pilot job, you can't be picky about the pay.

Also, when you get your first pilot job, the money doesn't really matter as long as you can survive—you are mostly working to build flight hours and gain experience. It's sad, but true.

Even your first passenger airline or cargo job may not pay much during the first few years. Also, pilots flying piston aircraft in general don't earn as much as pilots flying jet aircraft, which is good to keep in mind if making more money is your goal. Just be aware that it may take a long time until you start earning the big bucks in a well-paying pilot job.

This type of progression is, of course, the norm with most professional careers — you start at the bottom with a minimal salary but eventually, as your knowledge and experience increase, so do your status and salary.

MEDICAL PROBLEMS CAN DESTROY YOUR CAREER

As a commercial or airline transport pilot, you will be subjected to a medical examination every six or 12 months, depending on your age and the type of air transportation work you are doing.

If you are over 40 and work for an airline, you would have to do a medical check every six months. In my case, even after turning 40 in less than a year of this writing, I need a medical check only every 12 months because of the type of flight operations we conduct.

But because I fly planes that are registered in two different countries, requiring me to use two different pilot licenses, I have to do both an FAA and a CAAC medical exam every year. That's still two separate medical exams every year!

While regular medical checkups are important to ensure that you're healthy for both personal and professional reasons, these particular medical exams can be very stressful. If the doctor finds something wrong with you, you are in danger of losing your pilot license (and thus, of losing your job).

Suddenly losing both your job and your career because of a medical condition can be devastating. And it can happen to any pilot, for reasons that might not affect other professions.

These reasons can include things such as high blood pressure, diabetes, sleep disorders, problems with your hearing or vision, and so on. They can be issues that you wouldn't even aware of prior to undergoing a medical check. Then again, that gives you good motivation to live a healthy lifestyle!

Having an Insurance Can Help

While it may be devastating if you suddenly had to stop flying, the good news is that the financial effect it would cause may not have to be so serious. There are pilot license insurance coverages available for professional pilots that could help you survive financially if something were to prevent you from flying.

We'll talk more about pilots' medical requirements later in this book.

CONSTANT STUDYING

Many people find it surprising how fast you can become a professional pilot. If you choose the right place and school for your training, you could become a commercial pilot within six to 12 months from your starting date.

It took me about one year of training, starting with zero flight hours, to become a certified flight instructor.

And I know people who finished the same course in six to eight months.

You don't need a four-year college degree to become a pilot, but you will need to devote a lot of time to continuing education throughout your career. For example, you will need to study manuals for all the different types of aircraft that you fly.

They are usually thick, challenging, technical manuals written by engineers and lawyers. Although these manuals may not offer the most exciting reading experience, they do provide value with the knowledge you gain.

You may also have to complete recurrent training every six or 12 months. Often, the recurrent training means you have to study the same things over and over again. It can be very repetitive, but it's necessary for aviation safety.

In addition, you'll have to stay current with new aviation technologies and changing aviation rules. All this requires significant diligence from every pilot. This work is what keeps the skies safe.

Studying is not necessarily a downside of the job, especially if you have a curious mind and a passion for aviation. And I suppose constant studying is a part of every professional career. Just keep in mind that the studying doesn't end when you get your commercial pilot license—it's only the beginning.

DIFFICULT WORK SCHEDULES

Pilots' work schedules can vary significantly based on job type and company. It's not uncommon for airline pilots to wear their uniforms for 12 hours or more in a day. Duty and flight-time regulations vary based on the type of flight operations and the number of pilots on board.

My normal duty day is 14 hours long with a two-pilot crew. For longer trips, we can add a third pilot and increase our duty day to 16 hours. With a fourth pilot, we could be working up to 22 hours per day. Regularly working such long days can become very tiring.

Regional airline pilots flying short-run routes may easily fly 20 or more legs in a single week. Some days, you may have to get up at four in the morning to prepare for an early flight. Some days, you may not get to bed until two in the morning. Some weeks, you may end up doing multi-day trips away from home; other weeks, you might get to go home every night.

It's an ever-changing schedule that might take some time to get used to. In fact, you may never get used to it. Schedules can even become much worse if you commute and don't live near your base airport.

If you end up working for a cargo airline, you may have to fly at night most of the time. Cargo airlines usually operate at night, when passenger airlines are on the ground. Flying at night can be a lot of fun for a while, but it may not be such a healthy way to live in the long run.

You can expect to work hard and have difficult schedules for your first few years as an airline pilot. But things usually improve with seniority.

The most senior airline pilots can typically choose schedules based on their preferences. Also, if you end up flying long-haul flights, you may only have to work a couple of flights per week—that can make the job a lot easier.

SLEEP PROBLEMS

Because of the unstable schedules, you might experience trouble sleeping at some point during your career. It's very possible, especially in the early years, that you'll have a constantly-changing schedule that will interfere with your circadian rhythm. And whenever you travel across time zones, you will have to deal with jet lag.

While there are a number of steps you can take to

reduce the effects of jet lag, it still takes several days for the body to fully adjust to new time zones. If you travel to different time zones frequently, your body rarely has time to properly adapt. This can make it difficult to get enough sleep when you need it, which can in turn cause serious stress in your life.

I have personally experienced significant trouble sleeping during my career, which is why I have studied the subject so thoroughly. I have tried just about all the recommended methods of coping with jet lag and improving my sleep. It's still difficult to get enough sleep sometimes, but in general I'm able to sleep well by following certain practices.

Self-discipline regarding sleep management is a must for pilots. You will be required to sleep at different times than normal, but if you approach it with a logical and determined approach, it can be a lot easier to manage.

If you're interested in how I overcame my sleep problems, you can check out my free booklet titled: *How to Sleep Better - 12 Proven Methods to Improve Your Sleep - and How to Recover from Jet Lag*. Get your free copy via the link at the end on of the book.[1].

STRESS AND FATIGUE

All of this can be very stressful. Pilots are responsible for handling multimillion-dollar machines carrying hundreds of passengers safely through the sky. While most pilots embrace these responsibilities, it can also be too stressful for many to handle.

If you experience the above-mentioned sleep problems, difficult work schedules, or issues with your personal relationships, the stress can become unbearable.

All this can lead to fatigue, which is a *serious* problem among airline pilots. And the pilot shortage is not helping the situation. Due to the lack of available pilots, many crews end up constantly working long days that are close to the legal duty-day limits (i.e., the maximum amount of time you're allowed to be in the air).

When pilots experience fatigue, it can seriously impact their decision-making capacity—which can impact the safety of the flight.

Long-term stress and fatigue can start to become a health hazard before you even realize it. All this can cause some pilots to resort to unhealthy habits, such as alcohol abuse.

Not only can choices like this cost you your career, they can also endanger the safety of your passengers. More than a few pilots have unnecessarily destroyed their careers with alcohol rather than seeking help dealing with the challenges that are associated with aviation. That's something to keep in mind early on.

Even without consuming alcohol, fatigued pilots are known to perform poorly. In fact, the effects of tiredness are similar to those of intoxication. Fatigue is extremely dangerous and all pilots need to be aware of how it impacts their ability to fly safely.

COSMIC IONIZING RADIATION

This is a topic I was hesitating to include in this book. I don't want to worry you, and I don't think this should stop you from becoming a pilot. But I decided you deserve to be aware of the cosmic radiation that pilots (and passengers) are exposed to at high altitudes.

Cosmic ionizing radiation is essentially rays from the sun and space that crash into molecules in the atmosphere causing particle decay and radiation. This radiation goes straight through the aircraft structure and is believed to increase the risk of cancer in humans and cause other health problems later in life. It's different from the UV rays that can be blocked by shielding yourself from sun or by applying sunscreen on your skin.

Most pilots don't seem to worry about cosmic radiation, but I have flown with at least one pilot who purposefully wanted to fly at lower altitudes because of his radiation concerns.

Everyone on Earth is subject to cosmic radiation, even at the sea level, but airline pilots are subject to multiple times the radiation depending on their flight routes and altitudes. That's because at high altitudes we don't have the blocking effect of the atmosphere.

According to one NASA study[2], a crew flying a long-haul London to Tokyo route for 900 hours per year would get a dose of 5.4 mSv (millisieverts) radiation, which is less than a third of a recommended maximum annual dose of 20 mSv. Very few pilots will ever fly this type of long-haul flight for so many hours regularly, and the radiation doses are still way below recommendations. All the other radiation that people get from chest X-rays and other things would, of course, increase the total annual dosage.

The study also says that with the accumulated cosmic radiation dose of 5 mSv per year over a career span of 20 years, the likelihood of developing cancer will increase by 0.4% The overall risk of cancer death in a Western population is 23%, so the cosmic radiation exposure increases the risk of cancer from 23% to 23.4%.

Doesn't seem like a huge increase in risk to me, and personally I wouldn't start worrying about it too much. It seems to me that healthy living habits with good nutrition, exercise, normal sleep patterns, and not smoking can go far in preventing cancer and other health problems later in life.

However, according to European Union council directive 2013/59/EURATOM[3] the European airlines are required do the following for aircrews with an effective dose of cosmic radiation exceeding 1 mSv per year:

- To assess the exposure of the crew concerned.

- To take into account the assessed exposure when organizing working schedules with a view to reducing the doses of highly exposed crew.

- To inform the workers concerned of the health risks their work involves and their individual dose.

So, there is some concern about it among the authorities. Also, my brother, who used to fly for an airline in Finland, told me they were provided with an annual radiation report stating how much radiation the crew members were exposed to each year.

That's why it's good for you to be aware of the issue

in advance. This way you can make an informed decision about your career goals — if you have a family history with cancer, you might want to spend more time in lower-flying general aviation jobs instead of long-haul airline jobs, for example.

No Reliable Information Available

NASA and other organizations are constantly studying the effects of cosmic radiation on humans (pilots, in particular), but there is still not much reliable information available about the effects. It's currently impossible to determine whether a disease or an abnormality is caused by the additional dose of cosmic radiation received from flying or by something else.

I didn't even know about cosmic radiation when I started flying nearly twenty years ago, but even if I knew about it, I don't think I would have let it stop me from becoming a pilot.

You can find more information about cosmic radiation from my resources page.

You can see there are many downsides to a career as a pilot. Luckily most of them are not so serious and you should be able to find ways avoid or live with them. Don't be discouraged by the downsides! For me the benefits of the career and simply the joy of flying are always greater than the downsides!

Chapter 2 Key Takeaways

- Perhaps the biggest obstacle for most people who dream of becoming a pilot is the money required to get started. Don't let it stop you just yet, though. In Chapter 6, I will talk about different ways to finance your flight training.

- In general, pilots spend countless nights away from home. This is something to consider if you have a family—or if you want to have one.

- Entry-level pilot jobs can be extremely low-paying. You might get stuck in a low-paying job for years, and at some point this can drag down your career motivation.

- Pilots have to undergo regular medical checkups, which can be very stressful. Every medical check is a matter of life and death for your career; you might lose your flight privileges if your checkup produces poor results.

- Being a professional pilot means you will be required to study *constantly*. Often, this means studying the same things over and over again. It may be tedious, but it's necessary for aviation safety.

- Difficult work schedules are a major downside for many pilots. They can cause sleep problems and other types of stress that leads to fatigue. Fatigued pilots are known to perform similarly to if they were under the influence of alcohol.

- You need to be aware of all the downsides that come with a career as a pilot. But don't be discouraged by them; you can learn to cope with each, and you'll learn your own personal limits as you advance in your career.

- Cosmic radiation at high altitudes worries some people but based on current research the health effects from are so minimal that it shouldn't be your main concern stopping you from becoming a pilot.

In the next chapter, I will discuss the different aviation career paths in order to help you understand your options and pick the one that best-aligns with your interests and goals.

THE DIFFERENT PILOT CAREER PATHS

Before you start your flight training, it's good to have some understanding about your commercial pilot career options. After all, working as an airline pilot is not the only pilot job out there; you can choose between several exciting career paths after you get your commercial pilot license.

Becoming an airline pilot is usually the goal of flight students, and for the non-flying public it's usually the only pilot job they know or think of (besides serving in the military). When I tell people that I'm a pilot, the first thing they usually ask is: "Which airline do you work for?"

When I first started flying, there was a period of time when I also dreamed of becoming an airline pilot. I had no interest in being a flight instructor. Although I was enrolled in a training program to become a flight instructor, I didn't even fully understand how I was supposed to teach other pilots to fly when I had so little experience of my own.

It turns out that as a flight instructor, I constantly learned new things while observing my students. The experience made me a better pilot. It was also very rewarding teaching students how to fly. Today, I can see why some people might want to make flight instruction a long-term career, rather than working in passenger transportation.

Currently, I have an airline pilot license but I have never actually worked for an airline. What you might find interesting is that I have never even applied to an airline job.

At some point, I just lost interest in working for airlines because I have been having too much fun with general aviation and corporate airplanes. That doesn't mean that I have completely ruled out the possibility of working for airlines someday in the future.

My goals and dreams have changed many times over the years. There were times when I wanted to fly crop dusters for the U.S. Department of State (they pay good money for civilian pilots) or seaplanes in the Maldives. I even applied to those jobs! But due to my lack of agricultural and seaplane flying experience, I never heard back about those opportunities.

There have been many periods in my life when I didn't know what I would be doing after a particular contract ended, or after a visa from a foreign country expired. But there has never been a period when I wasn't doing something related to my aviation career.

You won't have to decide on your career goals immediately. Just take it step-by-step and adjust your goals along the way. The most important thing is for you to get started and see where your career takes you.

DIFFERENT PILOT CAREER OPTIONS:

AIRLINES

In general, there are two types of airlines: regional airlines and major airlines.

Major airlines, such as Delta, United Airlines, and American Airlines, conduct international flights to destinations all over the world. They mainly operate large Boeing or Airbus transport aircraft that are designed for large-scale operations.

Working for major airlines is the top career goal for

many pilots. The credentials and experience required for pilots to work for majors are generally higher than for regional airlines, and the pay and benefits are typically among the best in the industry.

Working for the majors in the United States requires you to have a four-year college degree in any subject. Many pilots get their degrees through distance learning while flying for the regionals or while working in the general aviation field.

If you do your flight training at an aviation college, the training will take longer to complete but you'll have your four-year degree when you graduate. (We'll talk more about the different types of flight schools later.)

A college degree is not necessarily required by major airlines outside of the United States, so don't lose your hope of being a major airline pilot if you don't have the time, money or interest in pursuing a college education at the moment.

Regional airlines usually operate domestically and operate smaller passenger aircraft, such as Bombardier CRJs, Embraer commercial jets, or different propeller-driven airplanes.

These airlines normally operate under a codeshare

agreement with one of the major airlines. The job of the regional airlines is to extend the service of the major international airlines to smaller airports within a particular region.

You will most likely start your career by joining one of the regional airlines. The good thing about the regionals is that you'll be flying shorter legs and won't have to venture too far from home. At the regionals, you're likely to work long days for little money at first, but think of it as a stepping stone on your way to the majors.

CORPORATE AND BUSINESS AVIATION

There are more than 12,000 business jets registered in the United States. That's more than all the other business jets registered around the world combined. If you wish to fly corporate jets, it's good to have an FAA pilot certificate.

Business jets are usually owned by wealthy individuals or large companies. Some of the jets are fractionally owned by several parties that share the operating expenses.

It's very difficult for individuals to handle all the operations required to keep a jet airworthy and to have a crew available at all times. That's why there are jet management companies that handle all the maintenance needs, flight crew needs, flight permits, and everything else that's involved in private jet operations.

With a corporate job, you rarely work directly for the owner of the aircraft. Instead, you typically work for a jet management company.

The benefit of working for a management company is that you have more job security; the company may operate a fleet of airplanes, and if one is sold they can assign you to a different one. If you work directly for the aircraft owner and he or she sells the plane, then you're probably going to lose your job.

Corporate Pilots Rarely Have a Regular Schedule

All corporate pilots have different experiences with their jobs. There are no regular schedules or routes. You can be called to fly anywhere in the world on short notice. It can be a very fun and exciting career choice—especially since you often get to fly state-of-the-art airplanes that can fly in higher altitudes and at faster speeds than typical commercial aircraft.

I know I enjoy this aspect, and it's a big reason why I

think being a corporate pilot is the best job in the world for me!

FREIGHT AND CARGO PILOTS

There are a wide variety of cargo jobs available for commercial pilots. You don't usually need much flight experience to start transporting cargo in small planes. Cargo airlines utilize all kinds of airplanes, from single-engine piston planes to double-decker Boeing 747s or Airbus "flying whales."

Salaries for flying cargo are very similar to passenger airlines. The main difference is the "cargo" that you carry. With cargo, you won't have to worry about passenger announcements or evacuation training. Flying cargo can take a toll on your life, however, because you often end up flying at night when the airways are less crowded.

Still, I have met many cargo pilots who really enjoy their jobs. In single-pilot airplanes, it's just you taking care of business. And in bigger planes, it's just you and your co-pilot in the cockpit—there's no one else to worry about in the plane.

Also, there's no need to stress too much about possible delays. Trust me, the cargo won't complain (unless it's live stock). This is definitely a good career choice to consider—especially if you don't consider yourself much of a "people person."

FLIGHT INSTRUCTOR JOBS

As I mentioned before, most student pilots have no interest in becoming a flight instructor. At least initially. But I highly recommend you give it a chance. It's a great way to build your flight time and gain valuable experience.

Working as a flight instructor will help you prepare for multi-crew operations later on in your career. As a flight instructor, you will learn to fly with many different personalities, learn to notice your students' mistakes, and learn to work together with other pilots.

Teaching people new skills can be a very rewarding experience, and you might even want to make it a long-term career. You could even work your way to eventually becoming the chief flight instructor of a flight school. I can tell you from my own experience that it's good to be the chief!

Also, once you learn how flight schools operate, you could even start your own flight school someday. Being a pilot, a flight instructor, and a business owner is probably a dream combination for many people! Another great thing about working in a flight school is that you get to go home every day.

OTHER PILOT JOBS

In addition to the four most common pilot jobs listed above, there are many other pilot career options that you can choose to pursue.

- **Designated pilot examiners (DPE)** work directly for the FAA (or another aviation authority) and conduct practical examinations of pilot candidates. They have the authority to issue pilot licenses to candidates who meet the relevant standards. Becoming a DPE can be a logical step for career flight instructors. I was considering becoming a DPE in China, but there was an issue because of my nationality.

- **Charter and air taxi pilots** work for companies that provide on-demand flights to paying customers. This is similar to working in corporate aviation, except that the airplanes are usually less luxurious and you won't be flying with the same VIPs all the time.

- **Ferry pilots** are pilots who transport empty airplanes to new owners or storage facilities. They can work directly for aircraft manufacturers or for aircraft brokers and dealers. They also sometimes work as freelancers, transporting new or re-sold airplanes from one location to another. Probably the easiest way to get started as a ferry pilot is by advertising your experience on various websites where people are looking for ferry pilots.

- **Medical and air ambulance pilots** work for hospitals or local governments providing emergency evacuations and organ deliveries, and fly other medical missions. You could literally save lives doing this!

- **Law enforcement and government pilots** fly surveillance and transport missions for many different departments and agencies.

- **Agricultural pilots** use crop duster planes to spray fields with pesticides or other chemicals. The U.S. Department of State also uses civilian crop dusters for missions destroying illegal drug fields in some countries... At least they used to, according to my "sources." These are very well-paying but hard to get jobs!

- **Firefighting pilots** fly similar missions as crop duster pilots. Their job is to fly over fires on the ground and release water to help put them out. It could be very interesting, rewarding, and respectable to be both a firefighter and a professional pilot!

- **Banner towing, glider towing, and skydiver transport**: All these have their own associated challenges and skills. I can't say that I know anyone doing these types of jobs as a long-term career, but they are certainly good ways to gain some flight experience. If you're interested in skydiving yourself, then working for a skydiving school would be a no-brainer. The same goes with flying gliders—if you like to fly gliders, then why not get involved with a glider school or club? And I can't imagine a more relaxing pilot job than towing banners back and forth along Miami Beach.

- **Test pilots** are employed by different aircraft manufacturers, militaries, and other aviation companies. It can be a risky job, but getting involved in the development of a new aircraft would certainly be interesting.

- **Air tours and sightseeing pilots**: This is a fairly easy and enjoyable job, I would imagine. Get paid to take tourists up on sightseeing expeditions and then collect tips after the flight! (You'll rarely get tipped in other types of pilot jobs.)

- **Airshow, stunt, and air race pilots**: You don't have to be in the transport or education business to be a professional pilot —you can also be an entertainer or an athlete! Getting paid while having fun...

sounds good to me! The downside is that you would need some sponsor money to get started (as is usually the case in motorsports). This is also one of the most dangerous pilot jobs.

- **Military pilots**: All branches of the military have their own pilots who fly different types of aircraft and different types of missions. With the military, you could get your flight training and education paid for while also earning a salary. It would require years of commitment to become a military pilot, however, and you would be subjected to a lot of physical and psychological stress. But considering the rewards, it may be worth it. And after a certain number of years in service, you would be a good candidate for just about any civilian pilot job. Applying for military flight academy would certainly be a good option if you are ambitious enough and don't mind the military lifestyle.

- **Astronauts**: Yes, you could become an astronaut! Never think it's impossible! Never! Several years ago, I was seriously

looking into becoming an astronaut. I firmly
believe that anyone can accomplish just
about anything they want, if they have
enough determination and work hard (and
catch just a little bit of luck). While I was
studying for my bachelor's degree at Embry-
Riddle Aeronautical University in Florida, I
noticed there were some astronauts in the
alumni. I immediately got excited about
becoming one. On TV, I had seen astronauts
training under water in swimming pools that
simulated weightlessness. I had done some
training with the Finnish military, held an
advanced open-water scuba diving license,
and I was a pilot. I would be the perfect
candidate, right?! Well, not really, as it
turned out. In two or three clicks (about 30
seconds of browsing the NASA website) I
learned that NASA astronauts had to be US
citizens. So that was the end of that dream.

No other organization was conducting space flights
at the time, so I didn't even research the topic any
further. However, you happen to be in luck! More and
more civilian space flight companies are starting up. I
bet that in 10 or 20 years there will be much more

demand for astronaut pilots than there is at the moment. They even offer space flight degrees at Embry-Riddle now. I'm kind of hoping to inspire one of my readers to pursue a career as an astronaut, so here's a list of the current NASA astronaut requirements:

- A bachelor's degree in engineering, biological science, physical science, computer science or mathematics.

- At least three years of related professional experience obtained after degree completion or at least 1,000 hours pilot-in-command time on jet aircraft.

- The ability to pass the NASA long-duration astronaut physical. Distant and near visual acuity must be correctable to 20/20 for each eye. The use of glasses is acceptable.

Go ahead and live my dream! If you make it to space, please send me an email! Nothing would make me happier! If you decide to pursue an astronaut career, make sure you check the requirements early on. I don't think my bachelor's in professional aeronautics or my

MBA would do me much good in space. Maybe I should have gotten that engineering degree in Finland after all.

You Have Many Options

You can see how many different career options there are available for pilots. During my research for this book, I talked with a human factors specialist who has an extensive background working with airline pilots.

Based on his experiences with over 430 one-on-one coaching sessions with struggling airline pilots, he concluded that one of the biggest problems they had at a major airline (over 5,000 pilots) was the pilots' inability to make decisions outside the SOPs (standard operating procedures).

He went on to tell me that pilots with early flying jobs requiring more independent thinking and doing things on their own went a long way to building pilots with good character.

By these jobs, he meant many of the general aviation operations discussed earlier — operations such as fire-fighting, ferry flights, or freight jobs require the pilots to think more outside the box because they face many unusual situations that are not covered in company manuals.

While there is nothing wrong with joining an airline

cadet program if you have the opportunity, it's good to consider you may have a more rewarding, enjoyable and successful career if you spend some time in the general aviation field before working your way up to airline flying.

Chapter 3 Key Takeaways

- Many people automatically think of pilots as airline employees, but there are countless other pilot jobs to choose from.

- A college degree is usually required for pilots working for the major airlines in the United States, but is not typically required in order to work for regional airlines.

- Corporate pilot jobs can be a good fit for you if you're not interested in flying regular routes and prefer more adventure.

- Cargo jobs usually pay good money, but you may end up flying at night most of the time.

- Working as a flight instructor is an excellent idea for your first pilot job, and if you like it, you might even want to make it a long-term career.

This chapter covered the different pilot career paths you could follow. Next, let's see if becoming a pilot is a good fit for you in general.

IS FLYING FOR YOU?

"There's no such thing as a natural-born pilot." — *Chuck Yeager*[1]

Now you know about the benefits and downsides of a career as a pilot. You are also aware of some of the different career opportunities you will have as a commercial pilot. This knowledge, however, is not enough for you to decide whether you actually *can* or *should* become a pilot.

Although I think almost anyone can become a pilot, that doesn't mean everyone should. There are many social, medical, and other factors that can make a career as a pilot the wrong choice for you.

Before you spend your hard-earned (or borrowed) money on flight training, you need to make sure a flight career is what you really want to dedicate your professional life to.

ARE YOU MALE OR FEMALE?

First of all, your gender makes zero difference when it comes to becoming a pilot. Gender shouldn't even be a consideration in this regard. Still, I think it needs to be discussed in order to clarify any misconceptions.

There are still some people in the world who seem to think that being a pilot is a profession for men only. Even your parents or other people close to you might think so. And that may discourage you from pursuing your dreams.

While flying is a male-dominated industry, there are many female aviators as well. One of the most famous aviators in the world, Amelia Earhart, was a woman who flew in the 1920s and 30s!

When I learned to fly, my first instructor was a woman. And when I was an instructor myself, some of my best students were young women. Currently, there are women working in virtually every field in aviation—

as airline pilots, corporate pilots, flight instructors, and every other job you can think of.

However, still, only about 5% of all pilots worldwide are female. This is mostly because not many women are interested in aviation, but many airlines are trying to change this. EasyJet in the UK, for example, set a target for 20% of new pilots to joining the airline to be women by 2020. They even used to offer £100,000 training loans for ten women each year to help with the process. Unfortunately, this program seems to have been canceled due to the COVID-19 pandemic. You should monitor their cadet training website[2] for updates, though.

SpiceJet in India[3] has set a similar target to have 33% female pilots in the next few years, and Air New Zealand is looking to have 40% female pilots by 2020.

Most airlines have not set such targets, though. Instead, they recruit whoever is the most qualified for the job, regardless of the gender – which is fair for everyone. But because of the push for more female pilots, the opportunities for women are out there, and it's a good time for women to get into aviation. The only way to really reduce the gender gap is to get more women interested in working as pilots. Now it's up to the ladies to apply for flight training!

A word of caution, though, as a female pilot, you

may face discrimination based on your gender in terms of pay and benefits. Based on a study by Glassdoor[4], the pay gap between male and female pilots is larger than in any other profession.

Based on the study, discrimination certainly happens, but it's difficult to say how much is actually based on gender. In my company, for example, the pay depends on the type of aircraft you fly, and years of service — in general, the bigger the plane, the more you make even if you work the same amount of hours.

Also, in the United States, for example, the airline pilot groups are unionized, and their collective bargaining agreement dictates their pay, meaning gender should not make any difference. In other countries, this might not be the case, though.

If you're interested in learning more about women's role in aviation, you can visit the website of an organization called Women in Aviation International.[5]

MEDICAL REQUIREMENTS

Understanding the medical requirements that come with a career as a pilot is very important. You should determine whether you can pass the pilot medical examination before you commit to flight training. This way, you can avoid any unnecessary setbacks later on.

There are some conditions that can disqualify you from becoming a commercial pilot. But luckily, you can work around many of them; aviation medical examiners are allowed to place limitations on your medical certificate, which means you can still fly (even commercially)—just with certain restrictions that vary based on your particular medical condition. You can find a list of medical conditions considered disqualifying from the FAA website[6].

Different Medical Classes

In general, there are three different classes of medical certifications for pilots: 1st Class, 2nd Class and 3rd Class.

You only need a 3rd Class medical certificate to conduct your flight training or fly as a private pilot. A 3rd Class certificate is valid for up to five years if you're under 40 years old. Otherwise, it's only valid for two years.

A 2nd Class certificate is required to work as a commercial pilot. It's valid for one year for commercial pilot privileges, but it's also valid for five years for private pilot privileges.

The 1st Class certificate is the toughest to attain and is required for airline pilots. If you're planning a career as a full-time pilot, you should first make sure you can pass all the medical requirements for a 1st Class certificate—even though you won't need it in the beginning.

1st Class medical certificates are valid for 12 months for airline pilot privileges if you're under 40 years old. If you're 40 or older, they're only valid for six months. In either case, you still get five years of private piloting privileges.

Get the 1st Class Medical Initially

You should definitely try to get the first-class medical certificate on your first medical examination, even if you are not going to fly as an airline pilot anytime soon. The point is to find out if you can pass the exam and make flying your career.

The interesting thing is that working as a flight instructor only requires a 3rd Class medical certificate. If you just want to complete your flight training and go straight into working as a flight instructor, you won't have to undergo another medical check for five years.

Easy, right? But get a job with the airlines and turn 40, and then you'll be under a microscope every six months!

You can find more details about the duration of different medical certificates here: FAR 61.23 Medical Certificates - Requirements and Duration.[7]

Where can I undergo the necessary medical examination?

You can't just go to any medical clinic or hospital for an aviation medical examination. You will need to schedule an appointment with an FAA-certified aviation medical examiner.

The FAA has a tool that can help you locate an aviation medical examiner (AME)[8] near you. Not all the certified examiners are listed there, however. A simple Google search can be useful you if you can't find one in the FAA's database.

If you live near an airport with a flight school, you might want to just drop by or call them and ask for a recommendation for a medical examiner.

Most flight schools send all their instructors and students to a particular medical clinic or medical examiner for their medical checks. They can easily help you book a time, and can tell you what to expect from the examiner.

What if there is no FAA AME in my country?

Internationally, it may be difficult to locate an FAA medical examiner. As I live in Hangzhou, China, my closest FAA medical examiners are in Beijing or Hong Kong—meaning that I have to travel to one of those cities the day before my checkup and spend a night there.

It's not worth traveling that far just to see if you can pass the exam. You can just do a medical examination in your home country that covers the same requirements as the FAA exam; unless you discover some medical problems, then you should be OK. You will still have to undergo the actual FAA examination before you start your training, though.

Create a FAA MedXPress Account Before the Appointment

Before scheduling an appointment, you should create a free FAA MedXPress account[9]. Then fill out an initial application form and print it. The form asks you for some personal information, and it helps you determine in advance whether you have any disqualifying conditions.

As long as you don't have any of the conditions mentioned on the form, you should be able to pass the actual exam.

How is your eyesight?

One thing people always say when they learn that I'm a pilot is, "Oh, you must have very good eyesight!" Well, yes—having normal eyesight is important for pilots. But even if you use corrective lenses, you can still get a 1st Class medical certificate.

An unfortunate exception to this are the requirements for perceiving different colors. Glasses that correct a pilot's color vision deficiencies (i.e., their color blindness) are not currently accepted by aviation authorities.

Red-green deficiency is the most common color vision abnormality among people with some form of color blindness, and the FAA states that you need to have the "ability to perceive those colors necessary for the safe performance of airman duties."

In other words, it's necessary for pilots to be able to recognize light-gun signals, position lights, airport beacons, approach-slope indicators, and chart symbols that mainly use red and green. This is especially true at night. If you have a color blindness, you can still get a medical certification, but it will have a restriction that reads "valid for daytime flying only."

It will be difficult to have a career in passenger transportation with this limitation, it, but you could still work as a commercial pilot in many general aviation jobs that are mostly conducted during the day.

Take a Free Colorblindness Test Online

Many hopeful pilots may not even be aware of their color vision deficiencies. Before you schedule a medical examination, it's a good idea to take a free color blindness test online. You can take one at colormax.org[10].

If you pass the test with a 100 percent score, you shouldn't have anything to worry about. But if you can't recognize some of the numbers inside the circles, it's good to contact an aviation medical examiner beforehand and discuss what your options are. There are three different ways of testing color blindness, and you would only have to pass one of them.

Read Through FAR Part 67

The eyesight standards for different medical classes

are the first eligibility requirement under the Electronic Code of Federal Regulations PART 67[11]. Those regulations describe all the medical requirements for each of the three classes of medical certificates.

You should read through the regulations to get an idea about possible disqualifying medical conditions you might have. Do this especially if you suspect you might have trouble meeting some of the medical standards.

Overall, the FAA medical exams are very easy. I rarely hear about people failing them. As long as you don't have a history of severe medical problems, you should be OK. But it's still better to make sure you can pass the 1st Class examination before you commit to expensive flight training.

If you have any doubts about your health, you might also want to check the latest medical requirements and find answers to your possible questions from the FAA Medical Certification website[12].

AGE LIMITS FOR PILOTS

You need to be at least 16 years old to obtain a student pilot certificate, which is required for solo flight training. If you start your flight training when you're 16, the earliest age at which you can apply for a private pilot license is 17. Pretty young, right?

It only takes about a month or two to get your private pilot license if you commit to it full-time. That means you could send your 17-year-old son or daughter to flight school over summer break, and he or she would be an FAA-certified private pilot by the next school year!

With a private pilot license, you can rent small planes and fly around for fun with friends and family. And while doing this recreational flying, you would be gaining valuable flight experience to apply towards a commercial pilot certificate.

To get a commercial pilot certificate, you only need to be 18 years old. That means you can work as a professional pilot and fly for a living even at that early age. You would be free to apply to just about any pilot job that doesn't require an airline pilot license.

The minimum age to obtain a flight instructor license is also 18. Getting the flight instructor license usually helps you find your first pilot job, as there always seems to be a demand for instructors.

To get an unrestricted airline transport pilot (ATP) license, you need to be at least 23 years old.

I got my airline transport pilot license when I was 37 years old, so there is really no hurry. If you've set a fast-track goal to work for airlines, then it's good to obtain it early on. You can actually obtain an ATP with restricted privileges already at the age of 21. But if you're like me and plan to stay in general aviation for a while, then there's no rush.

What about the retirement age for pilots?

There is really no set retirement age for private and commercial pilots, as long as you can pass the regular medical checkups. But there is a mandatory retirement age for airline pilots.

For multicrew passenger transport aircraft, you have to retire at the age of 65 in most ICAO countries such as the United States.

This age is not set in stone however. Japan's civil aviation authority, for example, raised the mandatory retirement age to 67 in order to combat the pilot shortage[13] in Japan. And in many other countries the maximum age varies somewhere between 60 and 65.

You can still work in the general aviation field even after retiring from the airlines, of course. So it's not the end of the world if you want to work a bit longer.

Overall, if you're planning for a career as a pilot, I recommend starting as young as possible. But even if you start in your 30s or 40s, it may still be a profitable and rewarding career.

You Can Still Become a Pilot in Your 50s

If you're already in your 50s when you start taking your flight lessons, I wouldn't get your hopes up about working for passenger airlines—especially the majors. But you could still work as a flight instructor, or in other general aviation jobs.

I have trained students in their 50s without any issues. They were only getting their private pilot certificates, but I also know people who have become instructors in their 50s.

It's certainly not impossible to learn to fly at that age, although you may struggle with certain things more than the younger students. One example is study habits—if you've been out of school for many years, you may need to re-learn how to stay focused and manage your time effectively.

Unfortunately, many pilots who start flying even in their 30s do have substantial problems in obtaining the required standards during their (airline) simulator checks. If you do start at an older age, be prepared to work and study a lot harder than your younger fellow pilots.

Remember, though, that it only takes a year or so to get all the licenses. That means becoming a pilot can be a relatively quick career change if that's what you're looking for!

FAMILY ISSUES

If you're married or have kids, you better make sure your family is OK with having a pilot in the family. You may be thinking, "Why wouldn't that be OK?"

The answer is because it can be very difficult for pilots to maintain a healthy family life. In particular, airline and corporate pilots travel a lot and spend countless nights away from home.

On average, as a corporate pilot, I stay in hotels over 100 nights every year. That doesn't include the many full-day trips I take, when I leave home early in the morning and come back late at night.

It can be tough on your spouse if you're not home when you're needed. As a pilot, you **will** miss birthdays, vacations, graduations, and other important celebrations at home because of your job.

Pilots have a higher divorce rate than most professionals. That's primarily because of the nights spent away from home and the problems it causes.

Staying in nice hotels and visiting nice places can cause jealousy and cheating on both ends. If your spouse is the jealous type, or doesn't like staying home alone, then working as a pilot is something you should think twice about.

If you're in a relationship, it needs to be built on

mutual trust and respect in order for a pilot career to work for you. If you bring your family troubles to work and lose focus on your flight tasks, you may put yourself, your crew, and your passengers in danger. Even if you have a strong relationship, it will take a lot of work to maintain it.

On the other end of the spectrum, you may also have to spend a significant amount of time at home. This can take a toll, as well. If you stay home for weeks at a time, you may start to get on each other's nerves. This is especially common for corporate pilots; sometimes I may be on the road for several weeks, followed by staying home for several weeks.

Also, while it's nice to be home, it can get irritating unless you have things to do. This can cause stress for your whole family. That's why it's good to have hobbies. For example, I started blogging and writing so I would always have something to keep me busy, no matter where I am.

YOUR PLACE OF RESIDENCE

The location where you live can make a big difference in how easily you can get started with flying. Unless there is a small airport with a flight school near your home, you will have to move close to a flight school. Later on, you may have to move where the jobs are.

You may even have to relocate internationally. I ended up moving from Finland to South Carolina for my flight training, then to Florida for a flight instructor job, followed by Texas for an airport job. After Texas, I moved to China. Here in China, I've packed my bags and moved five times to five different cities. All this because of my career choices.

Of course, if you live in a big city that has flight schools and is served by regional and major airlines, you may never have to move. But it's good to keep in mind that many pilots end up moving a lot because of their career.

This is something you should discuss with your spouse and family. Make sure your family is willing and happy to move with you when you pursue your career. Long-distance relationships rarely work, I hear.

YOUR ATTITUDE, MOTIVATION, AND PERSONALITY

If your goal is to get rich quick, this is not the right career for you. It will take a lot of study, work, dedication, skill, and even a bit of luck to land one of the best-paying pilot jobs. I still stand by my claim that becoming a pilot is not that difficult, but getting hired by a well-paying company is a different matter.

Most pilots don't earn more than you would make with a typical office job. But the rewards are there in the long-run if you stick with the career and reach for the opportunities that present themselves.

If you want to pursue a career as a pilot, you should develop the right kind of attitude, motivation, and personality for it. Don't think you can just throw money at a flight school and become a pilot. You actually need the motivation and passion to work hard and earn all your pilot certificates.

You also need to be able to accept failures and setbacks. You might fail some knowledge or practical exams along the way, but with the right kind of attitude you will learn from your mistakes and keep going.

Did you know that over 80 percent of aircraft accidents are caused by pilot error (or human error)?

Yep, a lot of blame goes on pilots. (Although there are, of course, several factors to consider and the causes of accidents are not always black and white).

Many times, the cause of an accident can be mapped to pilot fatigue, a lack of proper training, or a loss of situational awareness. These are things you will need to deal with later on during your career.

You will need to learn to recognize your limits and make better decisions. For example, if you're too tired to fly, call in sick. Or if you don't think you have received proper training, tell someone about it and request more training.

Hazardous Attitudes to Avoid

The FAA defines five "Hazardous Attitudes" that undermine pilots' aeronautical decision-making process. These attitudes have played a big part in aviation accidents, and need to be addressed by each pilot. The hazardous attitudes are:

- **Anti-Authority**: "Don't tell me what to do!" — People who are likely to bend the

rules and regulations that they find
unnecessary.

- **Impulsivity**: "Hurry up, start the engine!"
  — Impulsive pilots are likely to skip reading
  important checklists and do the things that
  first come to mind.

- **Invulnerability**: "Oh, it's just a small
  thunderstorm, we can fly through it!" —
  These pilots think accidents can only
  happen to other people.

- **Macho**: "Gusting 35 knots, crosswind,
  raining, and it's night — no problem, I can do
  it!" Macho, macho, men (and women) are
  likely to take unnecessary risks just to show
  off their flight skills, for no better reason than
  trying to prove they are better than everyone
  else.

- **Resignation**: "Well, there is nothing we
  can do about it" — Pilots who give up easily
  after the first sign of a problem, instead of
  trying to fix the problem, undervalue their
  own capabilities.

Many people have a mix of all of these characteristics. These 'attitudes' are no joke. I have dealt with all of these personalities during my career. As a flight instructor, you learn to better recognize them. But more importantly, you need to recognize them in yourself so that you can avoid them.

I can honestly say that there have been days in my life when I have personally exhibited each of these characteristics. But luckily, with experience and education, you can tamp down the hazardous attitudes that are most prominent in you.

Don't worry if you recognize yourself as a macho or impulsive person, or if you give up easily and resign as a result of failure. The idea is that you need to be able to recognize these attitudes in yourself so that you can fix them and make better decisions.

Antidotes for the Hazardous Attitudes

The antidotes (basically, things you think or say to yourself out loud in order to improve your decision making) for each of the hazardous attitudes are the following:

- **Anti-authority**: "Follow the rules; they are there for a reason and keep you safe."

- **Impulsivity**: "Not so fast, think first!"

- **Invulnerability**: "Wait a minute... It could happen to me!"

- **Macho**: "Taking chances is foolish, you idiot! There's no reason for it!"

- **Resignation**: "I'm not helpless. In fact, I can fix this!"

For further reading about the hazardous attitudes and their antidotes, I recommend reading an AOPA article titled *"Hazardous Attitudes - Which One do You Have?"*[14]

It still infuriates me when I fly with impulsive types who like to skip a checklist and press the switches of a multimillion-dollar jet, going against the manufacturer's recommendations. All those years as a flight instructor makes me emphasize the use of checklists and always follow the rules—they're in place for a reason.

I recommend that you spend some time assessing yourself and thinking about whether you have the right type of personality and temperament to work as a pilot. And when you recognize some hazardous attitudes in your daily life, take a moment to apply the proper antidote.

That's your first step to becoming a better and safer pilot, and you can take it even before you start training! None of these attitudes are going to stop you from becoming a pilot initially, but you can make your life (and the lives of the people around you) much better if you work on any issues you might have.

Personality of a Pilot

Some time ago I wrote an A+ research paper titled **"Personality of a Pilot**." In the paper, I discuss things such as "Personality and Pilot's Performance" and "Desirable Personality Types for Pilots." You might find it an interesting read, and I'm happy to email it to you along with all the other bonus materials that come with this book. Link to get the documents can be found at the end of this book.

INTELLIGENCE, EDUCATION, AND PILOT APTITUDE TESTS

Think you're not smart enough to be a pilot? Don't worry. If you have the ability to learn to drive a car (safely), then you have the ability to learn to fly an airplane! Sure, flying a plane is much more complicated than driving a car. But it's all learned in a logical, step-by-step, manner.

When I first applied to flight school, I had to take a basic pilot aptitude test to be admitted to the program. Not all flight schools require you to take such a test if you're paying for the training by yourself. They are however required by most airline cadet programs even if it's a self-financed program. We'll talk more about airline cadet programs later.

In any case, taking a pilot aptitude test can be a good way to assess your personal mental capabilities, even if you are not required to take one.

What are pilot aptitude tests for?

The pilot aptitude tests usually evaluate your basic capabilities in the areas of:

- Logical thinking
- Memory
- Coordination and spatial awareness
- Multitasking
- Understanding technical information

- Staying calm in stressful situations
- Leadership skills,
- Communication skills
- Math and physics knowledge

It might sound complicated, but don't worry. There are many online resources that will help you study and practice for the test. And you shouldn't expect to get a perfect score without studying and practicing, anyway.

Taking a pilot aptitude test is something that can be learned, just like flying. Nobody is born a pilot—people become pilots through rigorous education, study, and training.

Video Games Can Help!

If you're anything like me and like to play video games, you have already somewhat prepared for these types of tests! Flying is one of the few jobs that can actually benefit from playing video games, because doing so helps with your hand-eye coordination, multitasking, logical thinking, and so on.

The next time you play a first-person shooter game (like *Call of Duty* or *Fortnite*) go to the settings and invert the Y-axis; you'll gain extra benefit towards flying, because that's how airplanes are controlled—

pull back on the stick and the nose goes up, and vice versa!

Of course, playing video games won't be enough to prepare you for the test. You'll need to know what to expect in order to ace the exam. Take your time and find some pilot aptitude tests online, and practice them before you take the real one.

Then again, don't waste too much time on them if your flight school doesn't require you to take one. While an aptitude test can give you a good indication of your own mental capabilities, it won't do much good when it comes to your preparation for actual flight training. For links to different pilot aptitude tests, take a look at my resources page.

Pilot Aptitude Tests Are Also Used in Airline Interviews

If you have heard anything about the airline interview processes, it might also sound very difficult and intimidating. Some airline interviews may require you to take similar pilot aptitude tests—even after you already have substantial flight experience.

So even if you don't need to take such a test to be admitted to flight training, you may encounter them from time-to-time in the future, when you interview for airline jobs. That's when it's time to re-visit those testing sites, as well as study some interview preparation guides (which are also widely available).

No Special Education Needed

You don't need any special education before you start your flight training. All I had was my high school graduation certificate. But you don't even need to be a high school graduate to get your commercial pilot certificate.

Of course, getting a job flying as a commercial pilot without a high-school diploma is a completely different challenge, and I definitely recommend you finish high school before committing to full-time flight training.

Doing so will make the training easier, and will also make it easier for you to find jobs later on. Also, many major airlines require their pilots to have a four-year college degree, so I wouldn't recommend skipping higher education just yet.

You don't need to be an expert in math to be a pilot, but you *will* need to be able to comprehend basic time, distance, and speed calculations.

That might sound difficult, but I can assure you that the calculations pilots need to perform are quite simple after you spend some time learning them.

Natural Curiosity Helps

Although you don't need much formal education to become a pilot, it certainly helps. But what helps even more is natural curiosity and passion for aviation, for understanding how things work, and for technology.

ENGLISH LANGUAGE PROFICIENCY AND NATIONALITY

For FAA pilot licenses, you need to be able to read, write, speak, and understand English. The same applies to a license issued by any other country—at least if you plan to conduct international flights. English is the international language of aviation.

Currently, each pilot flying internationally must pass an ICAO Level 4 English language proficiency test. It's an official test that you can take after you have your pilot licenses or whenever you need it to advance your career. I took the test for the first time when I started my corporate flying job — and my company organized everything for me.

You Can Get Started with Basic English

You don't have to be completely fluent in English to

get started with flying. My native language is Finnish, but I did all my flight training in English. I hadn't spoken much English by the time I started my training, and I had a hard time understanding the aviation words that appeared in my pilot training textbooks.

I had to use a dictionary to translate the words to Finnish. It was slow to study that way, but it was also the best way to learn the language. After a while, it started getting easier and easier, and eventually I even started thinking in English instead of Finnish.

If you're from a non-English-speaking country, I think the best benefit of doing your flight training in the United States (or some other English-speaking country) is that you will learn the language at the same time. If you do your training in your home country, you don't get the same benefit.

Learning Aviation English in Advance Helps

I would recommend, however, that you take a basic aviation English course before starting your flight training, especially if you feel weak with the language. If you have a good understanding of aviation English before your training, the training will be much easier and faster for you.

And when your training is faster, it will also reduce

your training expenses. With a good understanding of aviation terms, your training will also be more enjoyable and effective because you will comprehend new concepts easier.

I have trained students with weak English skills who would just answer "yes" to every question I asked. After asking them to explain how something worked, I would realize they had no understanding of the concept.

They might still pass the multiple-choice knowledge exams and learn to fly, but without a real understanding of the language it's impossible to grasp any deeper aviation knowledge, which might be essential to safety of flight. Don't be one of those guys — learn English!

Consider Online English Training or a Flight School Offering English Classes

Jeppesen is a reputable aviation company that offers aviation English testing and training courses[15] online. It's a good company to contact if you prefer to study on your own. Alternatively, I would contact my local flight schools to see if they offer aviation English training separately from flight training. And if you decide to train in another country, you should consult the flight school about English proficiency requirements before enrolling for a program. Some flight schools, such as the Aviator

College[16] in Florida, offer aviation English training separately and together with flight training. Schools offering English training are used for international students, which might make your training more enjoyable as you won't be the only one struggling with the language.

Nationality Not a Factor

Your nationality shouldn't be a factor in becoming a pilot. However, it may limit the places where you can do your flight training. If your home country doesn't have any flight schools of its own, or if the flight schools are very difficult to get into, then you may have to train abroad.

Many countries welcome international students to their flight schools, but not to *all* flight schools. Even in the United States, not all flight schools accept international students (or can't help you with the documents needed to obtain a student visa).

But the good news is that many schools actively recruit students from other countries, and are happy to help you with the required paperwork.

Training in the United States

To train in the U.S., you need to obtain a student

visa from a U.S. embassy near you. And you also have to get approval from the TSA (Transportation Security Administration) for your training. Many flight schools help you with all the required paperwork for these approvals.

So as long as you can provide proof of the financial means to fund your training, and that you have a valid passport, you should be good to go.

If you have any trouble with your visa, reach out to the Member of Congress who represents the area where the flight school is located. They have a team of Constituent Service Representatives who can contact the embassy and see if there are any issues holding up your application. Keep in mind that if you've ever been convicted of a crime in your home country (sometimes, even a small one), this could impact your ability to obtain a U.S. visa.

Each country has its own immigration and pilot training rules, so make sure you contact your flight school or the embassy of the country you plan to train in. They can give you more specific information regarding your situation.

INTRODUCTORY FLIGHT

By now, you have probably determined that nothing

can stop you from becoming a pilot. But there is one more thing I recommend you do before making a full-time commitment: an introductory flight (sometimes called a discovery flight).

Many flight schools offer introductory flights for prospective students for discounted rates. Some schools even require you to complete one before being admitted to a professional flight training program.

The purpose of these flights is to give you an overview of the flight training process, so you know what to expect.

Without prior aviation experience, the introductory flight can be quite overwhelming. But that's nothing to worry about. One of the main reasons for this type of flight is to find out whether flying is really something you want to do.

If the flight makes you sick to your stomach or frightened out of your mind, then you may have to reconsider your goals. But if you feel good and excited after the flight, and are still interested in learning more about flying, then you should keep going with your training!

How much does it cost?

You can expect to pay somewhere around $100 to $150, or maybe a little more depending on the school, for a short introductory flight in the United States. Or, you can apply for a free introductory flight from the EAA (Experimental Aircraft Association), an organization that can help you organize a free introductory flight based on certain conditions. Here is a link for more information about EAA free introductory flights[17].

Introductory Flights Treated as Flight Lessons

Introductory flights are typically actual flight training sessions that you can log towards your total flight hours if you decide to continue your training. And you can log it even if you decide to do your training at a different flight school later on.

I think it's a good idea to do this type of flight in order to make a more informed decision about whether a career as a pilot is right for you.

To schedule an introductory flight, just contact any flight school near you by phone or email, and they will be happy to help you. Of course, it would be ideal to complete this flight at the school where you plan to do your training. But if that's difficult to arrange, then any school will do.

For example, if you're planning to complete your training in a country other than your home country, then it would make more sense to do an introductory flight closer to home.

I will talk more about choosing a flight school in Chapter 6 of this book.

Chapter 4 Key Takeaways

- Your gender makes no difference in becoming a pilot. Ladies, please don't let the male dominance of the aviation industry stop you from reaching for your dreams!

- While it's important for pilots to be healthy, the medical examinations may not be as tough as you think. But you should make sure you can pass a 1st Class pilot medical examination before you commit to flight training.

- You can start logging flight training hours when you're 16 years old, become a commercial pilot when you're 18, and get your airline pilot license when you're 23.

- While you are required to retire from most airline pilot jobs at the age of 65, you can still work as a general aviation pilot for as long as you can maintain your medical certification.

- While it's better to start flying when you're young, becoming a professional pilot may still be a viable career choice for those in their 30s, 40s and even 50s. Although the likelihood of landing an airline job diminishes with age, there are still many other jobs available for older pilots.

- Pilots tend to have a relatively high divorce rate, so make sure you are in a strong relationship if you want to become a pilot.

- As a pilot, you may have to move frequently. Make sure your family is OK with the pilot lifestyle.

- It's good to do some self-assessment to determine whether you have the right kind of personality and temperament to work as a professional pilot. We don't want macho men with hazardous attitudes in the skies! If you feel that hazardous attitudes dominate your personality, you can use the antidotes to correct your behavior and still make it as a pilot.

- Your education before you start your flight training doesn't really matter, but it's good to do some pilot aptitude testing to evaluate your own mental capabilities for the job.

- English is the international language of aviation, so you better learn it.

- Before you commit to flight training, it's good to arrange an introductory flight with any flight school near you. It will help you better decide if flight career is right for you.

Next, let's see what kinds of certificates and ratings you need in order to become a professional pilot.

PILOT CERTIFICATES AND RATINGS

"It is possible to fly without motors, but not without knowledge and skill."

— *Wilbur Wright*

To become a pilot, you need to obtain several different pilot certificates and ratings. There is usually a separate training course required for each certificate or rating. You will also have to take separate knowledge and practical exams at the end of each course.

Some of the certificates I will discuss in this Chapter are mandatory for anyone who wants to fly for a living, while some of them are optional. Which certificates and ratings you need depends on your career goals and the jobs available to you.

In this chapter, I will explain the different kinds of certificates and ratings that are available for airplane pilots, and talk about which ones you should get in order to become a professional pilot. Knowledge of all the certificates will help you later on when it's time to choose the proper flight school for your needs. It will also help you better-estimate your training expenses.

PILOT CERTIFICATES

- **Student pilot certificate**: Required for solo flight training, and used to keep track of people receiving flight training. It has no expiration date, and you can get it for free before you even start your program. I will explain the process of getting a student pilot certificate in Chapter 8 of this book.

- **Private pilot certificate (PPL)**: Allows you to fly a rental or privately-owned airplane with passengers. However, you are not allowed to earn money for the flights.

Private pilot certificates are primarily meant for recreational flying or personal transportation.

- **Commercial pilot certificate (CPL)**: Required for you to fly for compensation or hire. This is it! Once you get your commercial pilot certificate, you can call yourself a professional pilot! And, of course, this is when you can start applying for pilot jobs that pay you cold hard cash!

- **Airline transport pilot certificate (ATPL)**: The commercial pilot certificate can help you go far in your career, but at some point you will need to get your ATPL if you want to work as a major or regional airline pilot in the United States. And even if you don't plan to work for airlines, you may need it in order to work as a captain in many passenger-carrying operations. This will be done a few years down the road, because you need a minimum of 1,500 hours total flight time before you can even apply for the license. You may not even have to pay for the ATP training yourself — an airline may help you get it when it's time for you to upgrade from being a first officer to a captain. For example, I didn't pay anything to get my FAA and CAAC ATP licenses. My company paid for my upgrade (which included travel and training expenses). In some countries it's not even possible for you to obtain an airline transport pilot license until you are ready to upgrade from a first officer to a captain. In these countries you may join an airline with so-called frozen ATPL and work as a first officer. You can get the frozen ATPL by completing all the required theory exams for the license. You would then obtain full ATP privileges once you complete a practical examination during your upgrade process.

Notice that I used the term "certificate" instead of "license" in these titles. That's because the FAA calls them pilot certificates. In other countries, they are usually called pilot licenses. Also, you will hear people talking about PPL training or CPL training, which refers to private pilot license training or commercial pilot license training. Whatever you call it, it's the authorizing document you need in order to operate an aircraft (with certain privileges and limitations).

PILOT RATINGS

Ratings are additional authorizations that set forth special conditions, privileges, or limitations for your pilot certificate or license. There are basically three ratings you can have added to your pilot certificate. If you want to make flying your career, you should strive for at least two of them.

- **Instrument Rating (IR)**: This is a **must-get** rating. Every professional pilot needs to have an instrument rating. Normally, this is acquired after you earn your private pilot certificate, and will be automatically transferred to your commercial pilot certificate once you get it. Instrument rating allows you to fly in low visibilities and through clouds. Haven't seen any airlines that have their planes avoiding every single cloud in the sky, now have you? Didn't think so. Even private pilots should get this rating, as the training alone will make you a safer and more skilled pilot.

- **Multi-Engine Rating:** This is the second rating you should get added to your pilot certificate if you want to fly for a living. Without a multi-engine rating, you are limited to flying only single-engine airplanes. You can get by with single-engine planes for a while if you work as a flight instructor or take passengers up on sightseeing flights. You could even fly those single-engine Cessna Caravans, taking passengers from island-to-island in Hawaii. But overall, you will be very limited in terms of your job opportunities. Most airlines operate multi-engine airplanes, so just get the multi-engine rating!

- **Seaplane Rating (Single-Engine and/or Multi-Engine; Optional):** Seaplane ratings are optional ratings for most pilots. There are relatively few commercial operators that use seaplanes for transportation (or any other operations). You won't be doing any long-distance piloting with seaplanes, but they are a lot of fun to fly. I only have a few hours in seaplanes, and I only have the single-engine seaplane rating. But it was still some of the most fun flying I have ever done. You can read more about my seaplane experiences on my blog, FunkyPilot.com.

INSTRUCTOR CERTIFICATES AND RATINGS (Optional)

Although all flight instructors are pilots, the authorizing certificate for a flight instructor is not a pilot certificate; there is a separate instructor certificate. The prerequisite for getting an instructor certificate is having a commercial pilot or airline transport pilot certificate.

You don't need to become a flight instructor if you think you can find another type of commercial pilot job after you finish your flight training.

However, I would recommend you consider working as a flight instructor before you start your passenger transportation career. You will be surprised how much you will learn from teaching students. Working as a flight instructor for a year or two will give you a good base of knowledge before you move on to better-paying pilot jobs.

The instructor certificates and ratings are:

- **Certified Flight Instructor (CFI) Certificate**: Required to teach students at the private and commercial pilot level. This also allows you to train other flight instructors for their initial flight instructor certification. The initial instructor certification is normally completed in a single-engine aircraft, so you will be limited to teaching only single-engine students— even if you have a multi-engine rating on your commercial pilot certificate.

- **Certified Flight Instructor Instrument (CFII) Rating**: Required to teach instrument rating students or instrument instructors. Instrument flying is such an important skill that you will need a separate instrument rating on your instructor certificate, even if you already have an instrument rating on your commercial pilot certificate.

- **Certified Flight Instructor Multi-Engine (MEI) Rating**: Many flight students skip this rating on their instructor certificates. That's what I initially did. A multi-engine rating on your instructor certificate is usually not included in many professional pilot training programs, even if they include training for a CFI certificate. It's good to spend some extra time and money attaining the MEI rating after you finish all your other training and before you move on to working at some other flight school. You won't be able to teach multi-engine students without it, and you might miss some valuable experience early on in your career.

GROUND INSTRUCTOR CERTIFICATES
(Optional)

Ground instructors are basically teachers who are allowed to teach aviation knowledge to students. They are also allowed to endorse students to take their FAA knowledge exams.

You don't need to be a pilot to become a ground instructor. And working as a ground instructor doesn't involve flying, instead you would be teaching aviation knowledge to pilot students.

The reason I mention these certificates is that they are very easy to obtain while you are studying for the other certificates, and they can be useful to you later in life (especially if you decide to work at a flight school someday).

There will be some ground training and written knowledge exams involved in getting these certificates, but no practical exams will be required.

Ground instructor certificates are issued without an expiration date, so they can be a good insurance policy in case you lose your pilot medical certificate for some reason.

There is always a need for educators, so it shouldn't be too difficult for you to find a job as a ground instructor if necessary. Ground instructor certificates will help you share your aviation knowledge if you have to stop flying someday.

There are three different levels of ground instructor certificates:

- **Basic Ground Instructor (BGI)**: Required to provide ground instruction for sport, recreational, and private pilot students.

- **Advanced Ground Instructor (AGI)**: Required to provide ground training for all other pilot certificates, except the instrument rating.

- **Instrument Ground Instructor (IGI)**: Required to provide ground training for the instrument rating.

I took the AGI and IGI knowledge exams when I was doing my flight instructor training. That means I can provide classroom instruction and endorse students for their written exams. If you take the AGI exam, you won't need to do the BGI exam because as an advanced ground instructor you can, of course, teach PPL students as well.

OTHER PILOT CERTIFICATES

There are other pilot certificates, such as **recreational pilot** and **sport pilot** certificates, that you may have heard of. Those certificates have too many limitations, making them useless for anyone who is serious about flying. If you only plan to fly for fun, then they might be worth looking into. But with those certificates, you will have even more limitations than a private pilot.

Chapter 5 Key Takeaways

- You need at least a commercial pilot license with an instrument and multi-engine rating if you want to make flying your career.

- An instrument rating is extremely important for safety and efficiency reasons, and you should get it even if you only plan to get a private pilot license.

- Don't worry about getting an airline transport pilot license just yet. Focus on getting your commercial pilot license and some flight experience first. The time to get the ATP will be a few years down the road.

- Becoming a flight instructor can be a good way to start your flight career. Try to get the CFII and MEI ratings done while you're still in flight school.

- Ground instructor certificates are easy to obtain while you're in flight school, and can be useful if you're unexpectedly forced to retire from flying.

———

Next, let's talk about the cost of flight training and how to finance it.

———

8

THE COST OF TRAINING AND HOW TO FINANCE IT

L et me talk about the expenses—which are the number one reason people give up on their dream of flying—before I tell you the good news about the different financing options.

COST OF FLIGHT TRAINING

Getting a private pilot certificate in the United States will cost you roughly $8,000 to $12,000. An instrument rating requires nearly the same amount of training, and costs about the same amount of money.

That means you will end up paying around $20,000 —plus or minus a few thousand dollars—for a private pilot license with an instrument rating. That's just a rough estimate; you might find more or less expensive schools. It often depends on the location and the type of aircraft you want to fly.

Since you're reading this book, you're probably interested in becoming a professional pilot– not just a private pilot. Professional pilot training program expenses can vary significantly from flight school to flight school.

Cost of Professional Flight Training Programs

For example, Florida Flyers Flight Academy [1]offers a commercial pilot fast-track program for as low as $35,195, but it only includes 116.5 flight hours (and most of that flying is done in Cessna 152s). A program including a multi-engine rating at the same school is offered for $42,936, and an EASA ATPL course would be $69,439.

A similar program is offered by another Florida school, Sunrise Aviation[2], for $42,664. Then, if you choose a larger school, like the ATP Flight School[3] that has many locations in the United States, a fast-track airline career pilot program would cost you $83,995.

Notice the huge price differences? That's because ATP Flight School also trains you to be a flight instructor, and guarantees you a job after graduation. That certainly might be worth the extra money to some.

I just mention these schools as examples because I am somewhat familiar with them; I am not endorsing any particular flight school in this book as I am not directly involved with any of them.

Living Expenses Increase the Total Cost of Training

Keep in mind that those costs don't include housing, transportation, or other living expenses. Also, the quoted prices usually only cover a minimum number of flight hours for the course; you might end up needing extra training depending on the circumstances, which will increase the costs.

Cost of Extra Training is Based on Aircraft Rental Rates

It's actually interesting to note that the above-mentioned Florida Flyers Flight Academy offers some courses at a flat fee, which means wouldn't have to pay for any extra training you might need! (Again, I'm not endorsing this school—I just found out about it during my research for this book.)

But at most schools, every extra hour of flight training will cost you around $200 to $500, depending on the type of aircraft you're flying. Aircraft rental rates and instructor fees also vary greatly between flight schools.

For example SunState Aviation[4] in Florida has rental prices that range from $125 to $197 per hour. At first, glance, those seem like low prices. But you need to add $75 to have an instructor on board. That means you will have to pay a minimum of $200 extra per hour of instruction in their cheapest Cessna 152 plane.

That's not too bad, actually. But it adds up quickly if you need several extra hours of training.

Additional Expenses from Training Materials

In addition to training costs, you will need to have some money set aside for training materials such as books, charts, flight computers, a headset, and so on. Some training schools include headsets and all other materials in the course price, but at other schools you may have to purchase your own materials and equipment.

Exact Price Depends on Many Factors

At any rate, you are more likely to spend around $100,000 for your flight training and living expenses if you decide to do one of the full-time professional pilot courses that include flight instructor training.

That's a lot of money to spend on a 12-month program. The exact price depends on many factors, of course, and if you're creative with your daily and monthly expenses then you can definitely bring down the total cost.

The prices mentioned are just examples, and I'm sure there are both cheaper and more expensive schools around. If you attend a four-year college's flight program, the cost will definitely be more expensive, but you will also get a degree and deeper knowledge about the aviation industry, which is something to consider.

The cost of your training also depends on your training needs. At first, you might only want a commercial pilot license with an instrument rating. Or you might want to add a multi-engine rating to the license. Or you might want to go all the way and become a certified flight instructor with an instrument and multi-engine rating.

You can see how all this adds up, right? And the expenses will also vary based on the aircraft types you will use for the training.

There are simply too many variables to give you any specific information about the expenses you will face. It's better for you to do your own research on individual flight schools once you decide what you want to accomplish. More about different types of flight schools is included in Chapter 7 of this book.

Airline Cadet Programs

If you are interested in only airline flying, then you should look into airline cadet programs, which are usually even more expensive.

Some airlines offer cadet programs that involve training from zero hours up to a commercial pilot or frozen ATP level. Depending on the airline, the cadet programs may also include flight-instructor training or an aircraft type rating training.

Otherwise, the training and certifications you receive from airline cadet training programs are basically the same as you would receive from any other flight school. The main difference is that you would focus more on multi-crew and airline type of operations instead of single pilot operations.

These programs are usually difficult to get into, and the application process may involve a round of interviews and pilot aptitude tests.

In some countries the training may be paid by the airline, so I suggest you spend some time researching the airlines in your country. But most cadet programs are self-financed.

American Airlines[5], for example offers a program that would cost you upwards from $79,185, and JetBlue[6] Airways has a cadet program costing $110,000. The British Airways[7] has a self-funded ATPL training program operated by a partner school L3 Airline Academy[8]. The prices are available upon enquiry.

You can find many more airlines offering cadet programs from pilotcareercentre.com/Cadet-Programs[9] or by searching the internet. If your preferred airline doesn't come up in your search results, I would recommend researching the airline's website or contacting them directly.

Although the cadet programs are more expensive than traditional flight schools, they can be very beneficial. These programs usually come with a job guarantee upon graduation, or you will at least have an opportunity for an interview with the airline.

For example, if you complete the cadet program offered by JetBlue Airways, you would first be employed as a flight instructor before moving on to a first officer position with the company. With British Airways you would be offered a contract to work as a British Airways first officer. And pilot cadets graduating from the American Airlines program would "have the opportunity to interview at American's three regional subsidiary airlines" — as is stated on the cadet program website.

Eagle Jet Airline Pilot Program

Another airline pilot program that deserves mentioning is the one offered by Eagle Jet International. Eagle Jet International trains both FAA and EASA pilots in the United States.

Its FAA pilot program[10] would cost you $84,200 to $125,700, and that would include up to 1,250 hours actual work experience as a first officer flying a turbo-prop or turbojet aircraft.

EASA programs[11] at Eagle Jet range from €75,600 to €126,100 or about $91,555 to $152,840 (February 2021 exchange rate). They are more expensive because they also include EASA-specific Jet Orientation Course (JOC) and Multi-Crew Coordination (MCC) course. The more expensive EASA program also guarantees employment as a Boeing 737 or Airbus 320 first officer after graduation.

The Pay-to-Fly-Scheme

Eagle Jet also has a "pay-to-fly[12]" program. If you have your mind set to become an airline pilot as fast as possible (and you can't get into any airline cadet program), then you might be looking at even more expense — after you have your commercial pilot license.

As crazy as it sounds, some people actually pay for the opportunity to work as a pilot. With Eagle Jet you could pay to be trained in certain type of aircraft, and then you would fly the same aircraft in actual passenger transport operations, with or without a small salary. You can quickly gain valuable airline experience this way after you have your pilot licenses, but it would cost you.

To fly 500 hours in an Embraer ERJ145 aircraft, for example, would cost you an additional $55,000, or to operate as a B737NG first officer in Europe would cost you €44,500, or about $50,000.

"Pay to fly" is not something I endorse, and it's criticized by most pilots who work hard to get to the airlines through more traditional ways. But it's a way for those with money to get ahead with their careers fast.

And it's good for you to be aware of this type of operation so you know how some people get airline jobs. You should only consider spending money for this if all your attempts to land at an airline job fail. With the current pilot shortage, you should be able to find better ways to gain experience.

No matter who pays for the training and what type of training program you choose, it's a lot of money! That's the bad news.

Now for the good news: there are many options for financing your training, and it's an investment in your future that should pay itself back multiple times over—if you put in the effort and play your cards right!

FINANCE OPTIONS FOR FLIGHT TRAINING

Now for the big question: how are you going to finance your flight training? For many people, financing is probably the biggest obstacle in stopping them from ever pursuing a career as a pilot. It can feel overwhelmingly expensive to go to flight school. Most people simply can't afford it. But maybe you can find a way. Let's take a look at your options.

Unfortunately, some of the finance options covered here are only available for U.S. citizens. However, I urge you to do research in your home country and learn about the specific financial support options available to you.

FEDERAL GRANTS AND LOANS

If you are a U.S. citizen, you may be able to finance all or part of your flight training through federal grants and loans.

Some Flight Schools Are Approved for Federal Aid

Not all flight schools are approved for federal student grants or loans, but some are. Before you apply for grants and loans, you should choose the flight school where you want to train and determine whether the school is approved for those aid programs.

Specifically, research the school's website and see if it's approved for "Title IV Federal Financial Aid." As an example, one school approved for the aid is Aviator College in Florida[13].

If you can't find financial aid information from the school's website, you should give them a call. Or you can try to find the school's information in the federal student aid database[14]. https://fafsa.ed.gov/spa/fsc/

Once you have determined that the school qualifies

for federal aid, you can start applying for the different grants and loans.

Grants Are Free Money

If you receive a *grant*, it's free money that you don't ever have to pay back.

The Federal Pell Grant is meant for students who do not yet have a bachelor's degree or a professional degree, and it can be used at some flight academies or aviation colleges. There is also another grant called the Federal Supplemental Educational Opportunity Grant that can be issued based on your financial needs.

Another federal grant that deserves mentioning, although it's one that's awarded for an unfortunate reason, is called the **Iraq and Afghanistan Service Grant**. It is awarded to students whose parent or guardian died during military service in Iraq or Afghanistan after September 11, 2001.

You can apply for the grants once per year, and currently the awards go up to $5550. That's not enough to cover all your training expenses, but it helps.

Federal Loans Have to Be Paid Back

You can also apply for federal loans. Loans you have to pay back, because... well, because that's how loans work. There is a low-interest student loan called the Stafford Loan, which is issued directly by the U.S. Department of Education (instead of going through third-party private lenders). It is the most popular federal student loan program.

Helpful links for financial aid:

- To apply for all federal grants and loans, start by filling out the FAFSA (Free Application for Federal Student Aid)[15]. https://studentaid.ed.gov/sa/fafsa

- For more information about federal loans, you should review the loan types at Federal Student Aid website[16]. https://studentaid.ed.gov/sa/types/loans

- And for *even more* information on student loans and grants, you should take a look at the U.S. Department of Education's website[17]. http://www.ed.gov/

FINANCIAL AID FROM AVIATION COLLEGES AND UNIVERSITIES

Most colleges and universities offer various financial aid programs. These may include loans, grants, or scholarships.

Some colleges have their own aviation programs for students aspiring to become professional pilots. They are the top schools where you can do your flight training.

Training at an aviation college usually takes longer compared to training at a normal flight school, but you will get a college degree at the same time. With a college degree, you'll have better chances of landing a major airline job sooner.

Each college has individual financial aid programs, so you should research and apply to them separately. Some of the top aviation colleges that offer financial aid include:

- Embry-Riddle Aeronautical University [18]

- University of North Dakota [19]

- Spartan College of Aeronautics and Technology[20]

For a listing of aviation colleges in your state or country, you should check out the following link: Bestaviation.net[21]

FINANCING FROM FLIGHT ACADEMIES

Flight academies are flight schools that offer professional pilot programs. They usually offer accelerated training for full-time pilot students. You can get all your pilot certificates from a flight academy much more quickly than you can from a flight college or university.

Some flight academies offer their own loans or other ways of financing to students. There's at least one flight academy, ATP Flight School[22], that offers help with full financing of your flight training program.

You can get a 15-year loan with no payments due until six months after your graduation. This loan has a very high interest rate though, so be careful.

Most career pilots will be airline captains (or at least first officers) in 15 years, so a long-term loan like this might be something to consider, even in spite of the high interest rate. Just make sure you carefully review all your loan options to get the lowest rate and best possible terms.

LOANS FROM FAMILY MEMBERS

Unless you already have substantial personal savings, you will probably have to borrow money from somewhere. Borrowing money from family members is a common way of financing flight training.

I started flying when I was 20 years old, so of course I didn't have the money to pay for it myself. And I didn't have any college funds set up, because college education in Finland is basically free; there was no need for my parents to save money for college. But because I wanted to move to the United States, I had to get money for my education and training.

I couldn't get a bank loan by myself because I didn't own any property and didn't even have a job at the time. Fortunately, my dad loaned me some money from his personal savings and helped me get a bank loan to pay for the rest.

Most Parents Are Happy to Help

Most parents are happy to help you if they can afford it. But for many, money is tight and they may want to keep it safe for their own retirement. Loaning money has ruined many relationships between family members and friends, so be careful. Don't push your parents too hard, as they are not required to pay for your flight training.

Be Ready to Sign a Contract

You should be ready to sign a legally-binding loan document... even if you borrow money from your own family members. If you do this, make sure you indicate a specific time when you will start to pay back the loan. And then, make sure you stick to the payment schedule. This will keep everyone happy.

I took more and more bank loans during my seven years in the United States because I had barely any income. I needed help from my dad for all of this, because I needed someone to guarantee I would pay those loans back.

I started paying back my loans immediately after I got a job making decent money in China. Long-term loans with low interest rates were certainly worth taking, as I now earn more money in a year than what I paid for my flight training and college classes in the United States over several years.

If your family needs convincing about the value of investing money in your flight training, show them your career prospects. Statistics showing the worldwide pilot shortage and some pilot salary information should convince them of the potential that exists with this career. Have them read this book to show them where the money is going.

Just remember, you *will* have to pay back any loans you take—even if those loans come from your parents! Unless they are very generous, of course!

PRIVATE LOANS AND CREDIT CARDS

There are many lenders that can provide you with financial aid. You can just walk into your local bank and ask what kind of loans they have available for flight training students. Unfortunately, most banks won't have any specific loans tailored toward flight training, but it doesn't hurt to ask.

It can be difficult to get a loan if you don't own property, have a high-paying job, or have an excellent credit history. If that's the case, you'll need a co-signer for a loan. The co-signer guarantees that the loan will be paid back. And if you can't make the payments on time, then your co-signer will have to pay.

As I mentioned earlier, my dad helped me get loans for my flight training and other studies in the United States. If you ask your parents for help, just make sure you have a plan to pay back the loan—you don't want your parents to lose their house if something goes wrong!

Financial Organizations Other than Banks

But don't only think of banks when you consider your loan options. There are several organizations that specialize in flight student loans. The Aircraft Owners and Pilots Association[23] (AOPA) is an old and trusted organization that provides financing for flight training (even for international students).

Another such lender is Pilot Finance Inc[24]., which actually specializes in financing flight training. Just be cautious with these types of lenders; the interest rates can be very high! For example, with Pilot Finance the interest rates vary from 9 to 18 percent per year, based on your qualifications. That's *a lot* of interest.

Credit Cards Are Also Worth Considering

In many cases, your personal credit card interest rates might be lower than 9 to 18 percent. So, please do your homework and compare the interest rates between several different lenders (and even with credit card companies).

If you only need $5,000 to $10,000 initially for your private pilot training, then it might be worth just using your credit card rather than taking a high-interest loan. But credit card interest rates are also very high, so make sure you pay them back fast!

I know many pilots have actually applied for various credit cards with the sole purpose of using them for flight training. With new credit cards there is usually an interest-free period, so as long as you pay them back fast (before the high interest rates kick in), you can potentially save money.

———

For a **list of different finance companies** worth considering, please check out my resources page.

In any case, I would first contact different banks and see what kind of loans they can offer you for financing your flight training. In countries such as Finland, you may be able to get very low-rate student loans that you wouldn't have to pay back in a hurry.

If you don't qualify for student loans, then you should contact several different banks and other finance companies. Don't take the first offer you get. You need to compare different interest rates, length of loans, and other terms and conditions before you commit to anything.

Once you get a loan, the financial burden may actually keep you motivated to finish your training quickly. If you focus all your time and energy on studying the textbooks and flying as often as possible, you'll be able to become a commercial pilot sooner and thus able to earn money while flying a plane.

WORKING WHILE TRAINING

If you already have a job that pays well enough to cover your flight training costs, that's great. You can just keep doing your day job, and fly in the evenings and on weekends.

Training this way will certainly be slower than training full time, but you won't have to stress about finances—and you can take your time finding a good pilot job after you finish your training.

Try to Get an Aviation Related Job

Working just about any job while training will help you with the expenses. But it's not good if you only have time for a couple of flight lessons per month. If you can't focus on consistent flight training, it will end up costing you a lot more in the end.

Instead of working at a low-paying job outside the airport, you should consider taking a job at a flight school where you plan to train. Or at least try to find a job at the same airport.

Working at a flight school while taking lessons has some benefits with regard to your flight training. If you're involved in flight school operations, you'll become familiar with all aspects of flight training.

The more familiar you are with everything, the less training you'll need in the end. You will also get free training in terms of the aviation knowledge you'll pick up while working in the field.

It might be better to train full time if you can find other ways to finance it.

If you're fully committed to a career as a pilot and you can find other ways to finance your training, then it might be better to commit to full-time training as opposed to working at the same time. Training full time can reduce the duration of your program by several months (or even years, in some cases). That means you can work as a pilot sooner, rather than spending more time at the dead-end job you're trying to quit.

However, don't quit your day job unless you are certain that you will have a pilot job upon graduation—especially if you must take loans for financing your training. Without a guaranteed job you may face some serious financial difficulties later on.

AVIATION SCHOLARSHIPS

If you qualify for one, a scholarship is probably the best way to finance your flight training. Scholarships are granted by different organizations and they provide financial aid for students to further their education.

They are awarded based on various criteria—typically academic or demographic factors, but sometimes other factors as well. Scholarships are literally free money—you never have to pay them back. It doesn't get any better than that!

There are tons of scholarships available for all kinds of schools and education, including *flight training*.

It normally takes quite a bit of research on your part to find a suitable scholarship, and there are still no guarantees you'll get one. But I have tried to make it as easy as possible for you by compiling a list of aviation scholarships that will be emailed to you with all my other bonus materials. Access the materials via the link at the end of the book.

Once you get the list, I encourage you to go through all the links and find out if you meet the criteria. Then, apply to each and every one of them! It won't be easy, and you are right to be skeptical about free money, but you might get lucky and have at least some of your flight training paid that way!

There is one specific scholarship that I want to mention here – The FunkyPilot Flight Training Scholarship. It's a scholarship fund that I started in 2020. You can find more details about the scholarship by watching the video at the bottom of this website: https://funkypilotstore.com/pages/about-us.[25]

I was hoping the video would have gone viral when I published it, but that didn't happen – yet. Basically, I started an online store selling all kinds of aviation-themed items, and a part of all my profits will go into the fund. In the video, I mention that I donate 100% of my 2020 profits into the fund; now I have extended this, and I will put all my 2021 earnings into the fund as well.

I'm hoping this will generate enough funds to sponsor a full flight training scholarships to at least one aspiring pilot every year! So, please check it out, and hopefully, more people get to fund their training through scholarships.

FINANCING THROUGH MILITARY BENEFITS

If you served in the U.S. military, you may be eligible to get your flight training paid for by the government. In some cases, you might even be eligible if one of your parents served in the military.

For more about financing through the military, visit the website of the U.S. Department of Veterans Affairs/GI Bill[26].

- https://www.benefits.va.gov/gibill/

You can also call your Member of Congress' district office and ask to speak with a Constituent Services Representative; they're well-versed in how to apply for different federal programs.

Once you determine where you want to do your flight training, you should contact the flight school and ask if they're approved for military financing. Not all flight schools are approved for it, but many are. You can find a list of a few flight schools that are approved for military financing on my resources page.

FINANCE THROUGH AIRLINE CADET PROGRAMS

I am not aware of any airlines currently paying for their cadets' full training costs in the United States, but it does happen in some countries.

In China, for example, airlines recruit their cadets straight out of college. The students have to sign a very long-term contract with the airline, but the airline then pays for all the training expenses.

I recommend you research whether your local airlines have any similar programs. You can normally find this information in the career section of the airline's website. For this type of program, the selection process will be very difficult. But it will certainly be worth the effort if you get selected.

Even though most airlines don't pay for the training, they may offer some type of financial aid. American Airlines, for example, works with a certain lender to make custom career loans[27] available for the cadets. JetBlue Airways offers similar help for its cadet program[28] through loans from either Wells Fargo or US

Credit.

Most airlines won't guarantee the loan, but you are more likely to get it accepted if you have been approved for an airline cadet program. Some airlines may help you secure the loan, which you would then pay back gradually through salary reduction. The terms and conditions vary among airlines, so it's good to compare your options.

FIND WHAT WORKS FOR YOU

As you can see, there are several possible ways to finance your flight training. Take your time, research sufficiently, and determine which methods will work best for you. You can even use a combination of some or all of the methods I have described.

Just find a way to pay for your training and it will be worth it! Don't let the initial financial burden kill your dream of becoming pilot!

Chapter 6 Key Takeaways

- The cost of flight training depends on many variables, so you should determine your training needs and desires before trying to estimate how much money you need.

- Training costs also vary significantly between flight schools, so it's good to research several schools before settling on the one that best matches your aviation goals.

- You should incorporate an estimate of your living expenses into your estimate of your flight training costs, because if you do full-time training you're unlikely to have any meaningful income during that period.

There are several ways to finance your flight training:

- Federal grants and loans
- Financial aid from aviation colleges and universities
- Financing from flight academies
- Loans from family members
- Private loans and credit cards
- Working while training
- Aviation scholarships
- Financing through military benefits

- Financing through an airline cadet program

Take your time and determine which financing methods work for you. Combine several methods if necessary—if you're truly passionate about becoming a pilot, it will be worth it!

In the next chapter you'll learn how to choose the best flight school for you.

9

CHOOSING A FLIGHT SCHOOL

C hoosing the right flight school is probably the most important thing you need to do before you start your flight training.

It's good to spend some time researching and evaluating different schools before you settle on one that meets your needs. This is something you need to do on your own, based on your particular aviation goals.

Once you have chosen your school and signed up for a training program, the instructors will guide you through everything else!

Before you sign up for a flight training program, you should research and consider the following:

1. Courses Offered
2. Possible Job Guarantee

3. Location of the School
4. Cost of Training
5. Curriculum, Course Structure, and Type of School (FAR Part 61 or Part 141)
6. Training Airplanes and Maintenance
7. Instructors and Scheduling
8. School Reputation and Quality of Training

Many of these considerations require you to contact the school by scheduling a visit or by contacting them via other means. You should prepare a list of questions to ask when you contact the schools. Use the same questions with each school so you can easily compare the answers. Even better, make a spreadsheet with the questions and answers.

You can start preparing your question list while you read through this chapter, or you can use my question list, that comes with the other bonus materials of this book, as an example.

1. COURSES OFFERED

Different courses offered by different flight schools may vary significantly. Not all flight schools have the equipment or personnel to meet all of your training needs.

For example, some flight schools may only have single-engine airplanes. That means you'd have to get your multi-engine rating at a different school.

Other schools may not have airplanes with the necessary instruments for instrument training, or they may not have a complex airplane (or a technically advanced aircraft) for commercial flight training. It would be better for you to get all your training done at one flight school.

Many small flight schools primarily train private pilots, but advertise all kinds of training on their websites. That may sound good, but unless the school trains instrument and commercial pilots regularly, their instructors may be "rusty" in those areas (to say the least).

In that case, you'd have to be extra-diligent to ensure your training covers everything required to obtain each pilot certificate.

Look for Professional Pilot Training Programs

If you're looking to become a commercial pilot, you should search for flight schools that offer complete professional pilot programs. They should offer single-price programs that cover your training from zero hours all the way up to commercial pilot certification with instrument and multi-engine ratings.

It's even better if the school offers flight instructor training, because that is definitely something you should consider doing as your first pilot job.

If your main goal is to become an airline pilot, then you should look into the airline cadet programs. Some airlines run their own training programs that are operated by partnering flight schools.

For a listing of airlines providing cadet programs, you should check out Pilot Career Centre website.[1] If you get into one of the cadet programs, you may still have to spend some time choosing a flight school. American Airlines, for example, has four partner schools: in Florida, Arizona, California and Tennessee.

If the cadet programs don't fit your aviation goals, or if you can't get into any of them, then it's more important for you to spend some time choosing your school carefully. Just make sure the school can offer all the certificates or licenses you're looking for before you sign up for training.

Look for Schools Specializing in Training International Students

Many   schools   also   specialize   in   training international students. If you're from Europe, you should search for schools that offer training for both EASA and FAA licenses. If you're from China, you may want to look for a school that specializes in training Chinese students and which can help you obtain the Chinese CAAC license after graduation. No matter where you're from, it's good to look for a flight school that has experience training students from your home country.

Also, if you think you need aviation English training, you should look for a school that offers English classes in addition to flight training.

Just make sure the school can offer all the certificates or licenses you're looking for, and meets your other training needs, before you sign up for training.

2. POSSIBLE JOB GUARANTEE

Many schools employ instructors who trained at that particular school. If you decide to become a flight instructor, it would be good to choose a school that normally trains their own flight instructors.

They may not be able to guarantee a job, but at least it would be good to know whether there was even a small possibility to get a job after graduation. One of the schools that does guarantee a flight instructor job is the ATP Flight Academy.

Some flight academies, like Eagle Jet International, guarantee either an airline interview or even a first officer job after graduation. This type of guarantee is usually more important if you decide to skip your instructor license.

While it's usually easy to find a flight instructor job straight out of flight school, it will be more difficult to find an airline job (or any other type of commercial pilot job) when you are a low time pilot.

3. LOCATION OF THE SCHOOL

It would be ideal to live near an airport and not have to relocate for your training. Unfortunately, that's not possible for most of us. I could have done my training in Finland, but it was more financially viable to do it in the United States. Also, it would have taken me a lot longer to complete my training in Finland because the weather and climate there is not exactly perfect for flight training.

Many Options in the United States

If you live in the United States, you have hundreds

of flight schools to choose from. There are over 5,000 public airports in the country, and many of them are home to flight schools. Chances are there is a flight school located within driving distance from your home.

Do a quick internet search for nearby flight schools, and then browse their websites or visit the schools in person to see what kind of planes they have and what kind of training they offer. But don't commit to anything on your first visit, other than an introductory flight; it's good to do more research and compare your options.

You wouldn't want to start training at one school and then change to a different school because the one you initially chose didn't provide high-quality training.

Any interruptions in your training program will increase the total amount of time and money you'll have to spend becoming a pilot. That's why choosing the right school is a very important step early on; you want to ensure that your training will progress smoothly.

Moving May Be Necessary

If you're willing to move, then you need to consider where you would like to live and what the living and training costs are in that location. While weather is a major consideration in flight training, the most reputable flight schools usually find ways to work around bad weather.

They are usually located at airports where the weather is good enough for flight training throughout the year, and may reserve ground training or simulator training for days when the weather is expected to be poor.

In general, the weather is usually more favorable for flight training in southern states than in the northern states. Flying in the north may come with regular delays in the winter due to snow, ice or long-lasting winter storms.

In the south, thunderstorms and hurricanes can cause similar delays as winter storms in the north, so the overall flying days may be quite similar. Regardless of the state, some airports may be situated in locations that are frequently affected by strong winds. Windy areas are usually not ideal for flight training.

Contact the School for Advice

The best way identify areas that may be prone to weather delays is to simply contact the flight school and ask about the average number of flying days per year at that location. You should also ask how long it takes for an average student to complete the program.

. . .

Rest assured, however, that the most reputable and longest-running flight schools are located at airports favorable for flight training. Otherwise, they wouldn't be in business anymore.

4. COST OF TRAINING

The cost of training is, of course, an important factor to consider when choosing a flight school. It's even the most important factor for many flight students.

You can usually get a good idea about the prices of training from browsing flight school websites. But there can be more to the cost structure than meets the eye.

For example, the price advertised for a training course is usually based on the minimum number of hours required for each certificate. In reality, most students require some extra flight training (especially during the private pilot phase).

When you contact a flight school, you should get answers to questions such as:

- How is the cost of a training program broken down? How much would it cost to get each certificate individually?

- How would I pay for the training? Do you require any advance payments, or can I pay in installments?

You should never have to pay in advance for the whole training. Insist on paying in installments, topping up as you go. Many schools (especially smaller ones) are known to run off with students' money or gone bankrupt.

- How much are aircraft rental rates for different types of aircraft? Does the rate include fuel and oil (wet rate) or not (dry rate)?

Note that rates are usually wet rates, but if the school uses dry rates, then you should check the fuel prices at the airport.

- Can I choose the type of aircraft I train in? Can I fit into the smallest/cheapest aircraft?

Yes, this is something to consider if you are a large or tall person; I once had a student who traveled from Europe to the U.S. for flight training. He had signed up to train in a Diamond DA20 or a Cessna 152 aircraft, which were the cheapest airplanes to fly in our fleet. Unfortunately, after arriving he discovered that he was too big for those planes. I ended up training him in a slightly roomier Grumman Tiger aircraft. There were no problems training him, but he ended up paying more for the training than he expected.

- How much are the instructor rates?

- How much is charged for ground training? Are pre-flight and post-flight briefings included in the cost of a flight lesson, or are they charged separately? How long is a typical briefing?

This is important to know because briefings are often an additional expense.

- Am I required to purchase any specific books or other materials? Do I need to buy my own headset? And how much do they cost?

You shouldn't be forced to buy any FAA handbooks, as they are free to download. You can also find links to tons of free training materials on my resources page.

- Are there any other expenses, such as examiner fees, landing fees, or online subscription fees?

Remember that you are the customer, and you should get answers to all your questions. Any company that doesn't give you straight answers should be avoided, don't be fooled by smiles and flattery. Cost is a real concern for most students and the school shouldn't be hiding any fees. Getting your questions answered should be very easy. If the flight school is reluctant to provide you with this information, it may be better to look elsewhere.

Get an estimate of average flight hours for completing the training .

After getting answers to your specific questions, it's also good to get an estimate of the average number of hours it takes a student to complete a particular training course. That should give you a better indication of what you can expect to pay in the end.

5. CURRICULUM, COURSE STRUCTURE, AND TYPE OF SCHOOL (FAR Part 61 or Part 141)

In general, there are two types of flight schools: Part 61 schools and Part 141 schools. Sounds weird, right? Yes, that's what I thought when someone first told me about the different types of flight schools. I had no idea what Part 61 and Part 141 meant.

The 'parts' that I'm talking about refer to the different parts of the Code of Federal Regulations (CFR), which is the codification of the general and permanent rules published by different government agencies.

The CFR itself is a huge document, consisting of 50 broad category sections that are called 'titles'. Title 14 of the CFR is called "Aeronautics and Space," and is also known as the Federal Aviation Regulations (or FARs), which are published by the Federal Aviation Administration (FAA).

Learning about the different FARs is an essential part of your flight training.

Everything we do in the air is structured to follow certain rules that are designed to keep us (and everyone below us) safe. Title 14 of the CFR includes those rules, and is further divided into several parts that describe the regulations for particular aspects of aviation.

Before you even start your training, it's good to know the differences between Part 61 and Part 141 of the federal aviation regulations. Part 61 is about certification for pilots, flight Instructors, and ground instructors. And Part 141 is about flight school certifications.

The rules under Part 61 concern all pilots, but different flight schools may operate under either Part 61 or Part 141 rules for certain training programs.

The main differences between the Part 61 and Part 141 schools are their training structures and their accountability for the training they provide.

Part 141 training is structured according to FAA guidelines, while Part 61 training is more relaxed. Also, Part 141 schools are accountable for providing high-quality training and have a minimum student pass rate of 80 percent on FAA examinations. Part 61 schools don't have such requirements.

Because of the relaxed rules that apply to Part 61 schools, their students are required to log more total flight training hours than students at Part 141 schools.

For private pilot training, there's not much difference. You would need 40 flight hours at a Part 61 school, compared to 35 hours at a Part 141 school. Most pilots end up flying more than 40 hours at this stage regardless of the school, so it doesn't make much difference.

The difference is more significant for commercial pilot training. Part 61 requires 250 hours, while Part 141 only requires 190 hours. This is one of the reasons why I recommend you choose a Part 141 school for your professional pilot training—you can usually do it faster and cheaper.

Part 61 Schools

It's very easy to start a flight school that operates under Part 61. If you're a certified flight instructor, all you need to do is buy one aircraft, find a student or two, file some paperwork, and you have a flight school.

Running your own flight school is a common dream for many flight instructors who enjoy the job and have dreams of owning a business. It was my dream for sure. Unfortunately, it hasn't materialized. Not yet, anyway.

There are no personnel, aircraft, or facilities requirements for Part 61 flight schools. They are not even required to have a structured training course curriculum or a chief flight instructor to supervise training.

Of course, it doesn't mean they can't have a chief pilot and a structured training plan; in fact, many Part 61 schools try to operate in very similar ways to Part 141 schools.

Training in Part 61 Schools Can Be Very Relaxed

Training at a Part 61 school is usually very relaxed, and you're often free to make your own schedule. You can do things at your own pace, without worrying about ground school schedules or comparing yourself to the progress of other students.

You might end up doing all your training with one flight instructor who, at the end of the course, endorses you for written and practical exams.

Part 61 Schools May Be Very Small

That's especially true at small flight schools where

the owner of the school is your instructor, your chief pilot, and the receptionist. At larger flight schools, you will normally do stage-check flights with other instructors at certain stages of your training, just to double check your progress.

At Part 61 schools, there is no required time you need to spend in ground school classes before you can take any required knowledge or practical exams. All you need to do is log ground training in certain subject areas and convince your instructor that you're ready to take your required examinations.

This basically means you will do one-on-one training with your assigned flight instructor, and once he or she determines that you're ready to take an exam, you will be provided with an endorsement to take it.

You may be able to choose your cross-country destinations.

At Part 61 schools, the cross-country training flights can be a lot of fun. During cross-country training, you fly to different airports that are located within a certain distance from your home base. At Part 61 schools, you and your instructor can normally decide where to go. At

Part 141 schools, you are usually only allowed to fly to certain airports specified by the school.

Part 61 Schools May Operate as FBOs

Many Part 61 schools also operate as fixed base operators (FBO) in other capacities. In addition to providing flight instruction, they may offer services such as aircraft fueling and parking. Or they might offer sightseeing flights and aircraft rentals to the public. Flight training may only be a side business for these FBOs.

In a perfect world, every certified flight instructor would teach you the same skills in a similar way. But because of the lack of rules that apply to Part 61 schools, you may not get the same quality of instruction everywhere. It's good to do some research about the school's reputation if you plan to conduct your training at a Part 61 school.

Part 141 Schools

FAR Part 141 schools are often called flight academies. They normally offer professional pilot training programs that provide quality training at an accelerated rate. At these schools, you are usually expected to become a full-time student.

Part 141 schools need to meet certain requirements and standards set by the FAA. There are requirements for things such as training facilities, personnel, and aircraft maintenance. The schools also have to follow a structured training syllabus approved by the FAA for each training course.

Everything is Standardized in Part 141 Schools

Every instructor at these schools teaches flight using the same methods and procedures, so ideally every student receives the same training regardless of the instructor.

There is always a chief pilot who supervises the training, and sometimes assistant chief flight instructors (depending on the size of the school). In addition, there are check pilots who maintain the standards by conducting stage-check flights with the students at certain stages of their training.

For example, in private pilot training the stage-checks are usually arranged just before first solo flights, before first solo cross-country flights, and before the student is scheduled for a practical exam. At Part 61 schools, it's typically up to your personal instructor's discretion to determine when you're ready to move on to the next stage.

You may not be able to choose your cross-country destinations.

Cross-country flights at Part 141 schools are made to particular airports approved by the training syllabus. Normally, you will not be able to choose which airports you fly to. This can be a bummer if there are some places nearby you would really like to visit!

These schools have a responsibility to maintain an 80 percent pass rate for all students' practical and written exams—otherwise, the school might lose its Part 141 flight school certificate. That's why the training is strict and effective.

Stage-Checks Can Keep You Motivated

If the check instructor is not happy with your performance during a stage-check, they will assign you extra training. This usually keeps students motivated enough to prepare and pass the checks. It also keeps the instructors motivated to provide good training, because their teaching skills will be judged by their fellow instructors (and by the flight school management).

Because of this highly-structured training, the flight hour requirements are lower when compared to training under Part 61 rules. At Part 141 schools, you're expected to learn the same things in less time because you're following an FAA-approved training plan (and you are most likely a full-time flight student).

Part 141 schools can also offer some training courses under Part 61 rules, so don't count out a Part 141 school even if you can't commit to full-time training; you can sometimes talk to the school and work out a special custom training schedule.

Aviation colleges are FAR Part 141 schools that offer a higher-level college education along with flight training courses. Training at an aviation college is more expensive than doing so at a regular flight school, but in some cases it might be easier to get financing for college studies. Different aviation colleges have various options for financial aid, which can typically be applied to both your tuition and your flight classes.

If your goal is to work for a major U.S. airline one day, you may have to obtain a four-year college degree.

In that case, training at an aviation college would be a good choice for you. You can learn more about aviation colleges in AOPA's Aviation Colleges page[2].

6. TRAINING AIRPLANES AND MAINTENANCE PRACTICES

It really doesn't matter what make and model of aircraft you use for your training. You can do your private pilot training in a crappy old Cessna 150 or in a brand new state-of-the-art Cirrus SR22. The end result will be the same; you will get your private pilot certificate.

The same goes with any other certificate or rating. The only difference will be that if you did your training with the Cessna 150, you probably saved thousands of dollars of your hard-earned money, and your training was probably much easier because of the simplicity of flying a Cessna.

I have flown, in some capacity, 21 different models of light aircraft built by nine different manufacturers (Cessna, Piper, Grumman, Beechcraft, Aeronca, Maule, Liberty, Cirrus and Diamond). Most of them I flew as a flight instructor while training students for different certificates. Some of them I flew as a student myself.

.   .   .

I talk more about the aircraft I have flown in my blog's aircraft page[3].

I am proud to say that I still hold a 100 percent "pass" rate when sending my students to their practical examinations. None of my students ever failed a single checkride in any type of aircraft. And I trained hundreds of students from different nationalities, genders, ages, and backgrounds. The point is that you don't need a fancy new (and expensive) airplane to learn to fly. Any type of airplane will do.

It may be more enjoyable to fly in new airplanes with new instrument systems, compared to the planes from the 70s or 80s that have barely any instruments at all. But in my experience, I think the older Cessna 150s and 152s are probably the easiest airplanes for students to fly. They are very forgiving—even with hard landings. And with the high-wing design, you don't have to worry about wingtip strikes too much.

Then again, I flew my last 1,000 or 2,000 hours as an instructor in different low-wing Diamond airplanes. Those are also great for training. **With the right instructor, any airplane will do.**

Maintenance practices are more important than aircraft type.

Rather than focusing on the type of aircraft, you should make sure the flight school maintains its airplanes properly. Check if they have their own maintenance personnel and facilities, or if they outsource the maintenance.

Ask to take a look inside the airplanes so you can see whether they seem clean inside and out. Even as a non-pilot, you can probably tell the overall condition of the airplane just by looking at its different parts.

Are the tires totally worn out, or do they look new? Is the windshield clean? Are the seats and harnesses in good condition? Are there any broken knobs on the instrument panel?

Of course, none of this will give you any indication about how well the engine has been maintained. You would have to go through the maintenance logbooks for a complete picture of that.

But it should give you some idea about how professional the school is. Dirty planes with worn tires and dusty seats might indicate unprofessional maintenance practices.

Get a Tour of Maintenance Facilities

Feel free to ask for a tour of the maintenance facilities—and the rest of the flight school, while you're at it. Checking out the maintenance facilities can be interesting, and the condition of the workspace can tell you a lot about their maintenance principles.

You can get an even better indication of the condition of the planes by talking to other students at the school. They're more likely to give you honest insider information. Many flight schools have benches or chairs outside where you can watch the pilots and airplanes on the ramp.

Spend some time sitting and observing the flight school's operations. Talk to the students and instructors about the airplanes and what they think of the school. Just be friendly and tell them you're considering signing up for flight training. You'll get some good information.

As I mentioned before, the type of aircraft a school trains with doesn't really matter, but the school should still have a proper fleet of several airplanes.

Very small flight schools may only have one, two, or three airplanes; you can't expect to complete your training very fast at this type of school. That's because airplanes need regular (and sometimes unexpected) maintenance, and other students also need to fly. At a school with only one or two airplanes, you may not get to fly as often as you would like.

Bigger Fleet Is Usually Better

It's better if the school has a fleet of several airplanes, and even better if they also have several types that are assigned for private pilot training, instrument training, commercial training, and multi-engine training. With this type of fleet, you'll get more variety in your training (making it more fun and interesting).

7. FLIGHT INSTRUCTOR EXPERIENCE AND CREDENTIALS

Regardless of the school you choose in the end, you need to be assigned to a personal flight instructor. He or she can keep better track of your progress and build on it. A new instructor with each flight will result with him/her having to assess you first and then start teaching. Note that not all instructors have the same dedication and experience.

Typically, the chief flight instructor or someone else in the flight school management assigns each student to their respective instructors. This is especially true at Part

141 schools. The way students are assigned is based on how busy the instructors are.

There is nothing personal about the instructor-student assignments, and usually the students meet their instructors for the first time after the assignment has already been made.

Not all instructors teach the same way.

Although all instructors have the same instructor certificate and are supposed to teach the same things, they often use slightly different teaching methods. Additionally, not all instructors and students get along with each other. Everyone is different, and while the teaching methods used by one instructor may work with some students, they may not work with you.

Chances are that you'll get paired with a professional instructor who is able to guide you through all your training. However, if after a few lessons you feel like you are not making progress with your instructor, then feel free to request a different instructor.

Changing instructors is sometimes necessary.

It's not a good feeling for either of you if it becomes

necessary to change instructors, but don't worry—it happens to all of us. You will spend countless hours in a small cockpit with your instructor, so there needs to be mutual respect between the two of you. Even if you make mistakes, your instructor is supposed to be encouraging and motivate you to improve your performance.

A professional instructor should never get angry or yell at you. A flight instructor with a bad temper should find another job. If your instructor screams at you during your training, and you end up coming back from each flight miserable and with tears in your eyes, it's time to change instructors.

I once saw a student crying and an instructor cursing and calling the student useless in front of other students... situations like that are totally inappropriate and completely unacceptable.

You can be sure that instructor got fired (I was partly involved in making sure of that). And the student was transferred to me. I sent the student on her first solo flight a few days later with no problems—she just needed a different instructor.

There are some bad apples out there, but keep in mind that you can always change instructors if necessary. You are the customer. And anyway, the bad instructors are the exceptions to the rule; they don't usually last long.

Most flight instructors are professional and courteous. That's important, because flight instructing requires patience that not all pilots have. Those pilots might be very good transportation workers, though.

Choose Your Instructor

It's good to get some idea about who works at the school and who you should expect to fly with if you start training on a certain date.

By looking at flight school websites, you can usually determine who the chief flight instructor is and who the senior flight instructors are. But usually, the personnel change frequently at flight schools, so you won't get the complete picture.

A better way to get the information is by visiting the school yourself. Or, if the school is located too far away to visit, then at least give them a call.

When you talk to the flight school's management, you should ask questions like:

- How many instructors does the school employ?

- How experienced are the instructors, and what are their credentials?

- Were the instructors trained at this flight school, or hired from the outside?

- How many students are assigned to each instructor, and how busy are they?

- Which instructor would I be expected to fly with if I planned to start my training on a certain date?

Talk to Other Students

You can get more inside information by talking to other students at the school. You can usually find out who the most popular instructor is, as well as who the guy is that nobody wants to fly with.

The main thing you want to find out when you talk to other students is whether they are overall happy with the pace of training and the overall instruction they receive at the school.

Try to Meet with Instructors

After you have done your research, you should try to meet and talk with the instructor you think you might end up flying with. Even a brief meeting can help you judge whether your personalities will match. You can get a gut feeling about the instructors' attitude and professionalism, which is important for effective training.

When you talk to the instructor, you can ask questions such as:

- How many students have you trained? How many of them were PPL, IR, or CPL students? How many passed their practical examination on the first try?

- Why did you become a flight instructor? And what are your career goals? Do you think you will still be instructing here in a year?

- What instructor ratings do you have? CFI? CFII? MEI?

- How much ground instruction do you normally do before and after each flight lesson?

- On average, how many flight hours do your students conduct before their initial solo flight?

- How many students are you currently teaching, and how many flights should I expect to fly with you per week?

- May I talk to some of your current or previous students?

Other things to consider when choosing your instructor:

- Don't dismiss an instructor just because he or she is very young or new to the role; new instructors are usually more dedicated and motivated to do a good job.

- If you get the feeling that an instructor is there just for the short term and is constantly looking for better jobs, then he or she may not be the best choice. If your instructor quits in the middle of your training, it may cause delays.

- Also, if the instructor is too busy and already has many students, he or she may not have enough time for you during the initial stages of your training. It would be better to get an instructor who has plenty of time for your training, and who is always available for consultation.

It's your instructor's job to evaluate your progress after each flight. But I would recommend that you also evaluate the performance of your instructor. You are the customer, and you should be getting the training you're paying for.

Your instructor should be prepared for each lesson, and should provide you with proper pre-flight and post-flight briefings. Doing so shows that he or she cares about your progress. Your instructor should be ready to answer any questions you might have, and should even encourage questions.

So, my best friend is a flight instructor... should I ask him (or her) to teach me?

You are free to request a specific instructor if you know someone who teaches at the school. Just remember, the briefing rooms and cockpit are professional environments, so your best friend or a relative may not be the best choice as your instructor.

It may be difficult for them to treat you the same way they would treat any other student. They might find it difficult to point out your mistakes, and it may be difficult for you to take their criticism of your performance— even if that criticism is constructive.

I have personally found it difficult to provide proper training to other flight instructors who were already long-time friends of mine. It was easy to lose focus of the mission at hand; instead, we talked about other things. I think it's easier to do training when there is a clear student-instructor relationship. That doesn't mean you can't become friends with your instructor, though. I always considered all my students friends... although we didn't hang out outside the flight school.

Of course, every relationship and friendship is different. But in general, I would advise against training with someone who is personally close to you.

8. SCHOOL REPUTATION AND QUALITY OF TRAINING

The reputation of the school and its quality of training should be among the main considerations when choosing a flight school. Ideally, you want to choose a school with a reputation for producing excellent pilots with high standards.

That is difficult to measure though, and every flight school advertises themselves as being the best. Instead of relying on only the information you get from the flight school itself, you should try to get some impartial information elsewhere.

Who to contact for information:

- One option is to call the nearest FAA Flight Standards district office (FSDO) and ask about the local flight schools. They can provide you with accident history and a record of any FAA violations committed by different schools.

- You can also call a local FAA examiner who conducts practical exams in the area. FAA examiners are familiar with the students from different schools and can give you some insight into which schools usually train the better pilots.

- And of course, you should talk to the

students at the different schools and see how happy they are (or are not) with the training they receive. While students can't really judge the quality of the training because they lack a useful point of reference, you can at least find out if they feel safe and happy with the school.

To determine the reputation of the school, you should try to answer questions such as:

- How happy are the students? What do they like and not like about the school?

- How happy are the instructors? Are they too busy? Do they get to fly enough? Are they paid enough to stay motivated?

- Are the students graduating as scheduled?

- Have there been any accidents at the school? What were the reasons for the accidents? Maintenance issues? Poor training quality?

- Has the school violated any federal aviation regulations or other rules?

When I researched flight schools on the internet, I learned that some flight students write reviews of their schools on Facebook, Yelp, and other websites. You can find lots of good information by typing the name of the flight school + "review" and hitting "search."

Just take the reviews with a grain of salt, as it's usually the students with negative experiences who take the time to leave reviews; the majority of the students may be perfectly happy with the school.

Consider Using LinkedIn

Another good way to get information about a school's reputation is to contact pilots who have graduated from that school. If you have a LinkedIn (linkedin.com)[4] account, this process is very easy.

You can just type the school's name in the LinkedIn search field and you are likely to find hundreds of people who have graduated from the school — at least if the school has been around for a while. Then you can try to contact graduates and ask their opinion on the quality and credibility of the flight school.

CHOOSE YOUR SCHOOL

After you have researched your flight school options, it's time to decide where you want to train. If possible, try to visit your top flight school choices at least once or twice before you make your final decision.

If you're serious about a long-term pilot career, and if you can find financing for your training, then I would recommend you become a full-time student at one of the Part 141 schools.

But if you can't commit to full-time training just yet, or prefer to study mostly on your own at your own pace, then there's nothing wrong with training at a Part 61 school.

I can't endorse any particular flight school, because I'm not involved with any at the moment. Also, the best school for one person may not be the best school for another. There are many factors to consider, depending on your personal situation and goals.

In the end, it's up to you to decide where you train. But if you want a second opinion, or to consult with other aspiring pilots, please feel free to ask for advice in my Pilot Career Facebook Group.

Chapter 7 Key Takeaways

- Prepare a list of questions you want to ask from different flight schools. Use that same list with all the schools.

- When choosing a flight school, one of the first things you should look at is what kind of courses they offer. Try to do all your training at one flight school if possible to make it easier on yourself.

- The cost of training depends on many factors. It's good to prepare a list of questions about the training expenses, and then contact different flight schools to get a better estimate of your financial needs.

- Training at Part 61 schools can be very relaxed, and can be a good choice if you're only looking to be a private pilot. But if you're looking for a professional pilot training program, it's probably better to choose a more structured Part 141 flight school.

- The type of training airplane you work with doesn't make much difference with regard to the final outcome. A more important question about your training aircraft is whether it has been well maintained.

- A good instructor should always be courteous and professional. If you end up paired with an instructor who you don't get along with, you can always request a different instructor.

- Try to conduct some research about the school's reputation and quality of training, as this should be one of the determining factors when you're choosing a flight school.

Choosing the right flight school is one of the last steps in getting started with flight training and becoming a pilot.

Next, it's time to get started!

10

TIME TO GET STARTED!

I t's the final chapter. You're almost done! The previous chapters covered a lot of information that might feel difficult to digest.

Let me simplify things a bit here at the end. In this final chapter, I will give you **10 Step Action Plan** that should help you get up from that couch and get started with your pilot career!

Action Step 1: Determine Your Aviation Goals

Have you figured out your "why" yet? If not, **now** is the time to determine why you want to fly.

If you don't complete this step, you're likely to waste your time and money on what will amount to a very expensive hobby. Unless a hobby is what you're looking for?

Looking to fly for fun?

If you only want to fly for fun, then I recommend you just get a private pilot license with an instrument rating. You could also look into getting a recreational pilot or sport pilot license instead, if you're concerned about money. Just understand that those options come with more limitations than a private pilot certification.

Looking for a career?

If you want to make flying your career, then you should decide what kind of pilot career path you want to pursue. If your goal is to work for airlines, then you will need to get a commercial pilot license with instrument and multi-engine ratings—and you should apply to different airline cadet programs. If you just want to do some sightseeing flights at a local flight club, then a single-engine commercial license might be enough. If flying seaplanes is what you're looking for, then it's the seaplane rating you should pursue. And don't forget about the possibility of working as a flight instructor (at least initially).

Deciding on your initial career goal will make it easier to choose the right flight school. You can always change your goals later if you have a hard time finding jobs in your chosen field, or if your chosen path ends up being different from what you expected.

Who knows, I might even still change from corporate aviation to scheduled airlines someday...

Action Step 2: Evaluate Your Medical Fitness to Fly

Before you spend time or money planning your pilot career, you should determine whether you are medically fit to fly.

- **First**, read through the Electronic Code of Federal Regulations PART 67, which describes the medical standards for pilots. If you think you can meet all the standards and don't have any disqualifying conditions, you can move on to next step.

- **Next**, go ahead and create a free FAA MedXPress account, fill out an initial application form, and print it. This is the form you need to bring with you to the clinic when you do your medical examination.

- **And then**, you need to locate an aviation medical examiner (AME) using the FAA AME locator. If you can't find one near you, I recommend a quick Google search to find one—or just ask any nearby flight school for recommendations.

- **Now you're ready** to schedule a 1st Class medical examination with the AME you chose. Once you have passed the medical exam, you can be assured that you can become a pilot. Go ahead to Action Step 3.

Don't lose hope even if you fail the medical examination.

If you fail the examination for some reason, then you should discuss your options with the doctor. You might be able to get a medical certificate with some limitations, or maybe your problem can be fixed through medication or other means.

For example, if your blood pressure is too high, you might be able to reduce it by changing your living habits (such as eating better and exercising more).

Action Step 3: Take Care of Any Family Issues

Most people are very excited by the prospect of having a pilot in the family—and even about being married to one. But the reality of having a pilot around is usually not that rosy.

Pilots travel a lot and spend countless nights away from home, which can cause major issues in relationships.

Make sure your spouse is:

- OK with you committing to a pilot career.

- Make sure he or she is OK with the possibility that you may sometimes spend as much as a month away from home because of training.

- Make sure he or she is OK with the fact that

you will be away from home 100 nights (or more) per year.

- Make sure he or she is OK with the fact that you might even have to move out of the country at some point in the future.

And what if it's not OK with your spouse? Should you give up your dream of becoming a pilot or break-off the relationship in order to pursue your love of flight?

Well, for some people it may come to that. But first, I recommend you go back to Step 1 and consider some of the pilot jobs that don't require so much travel.

Working for a local flight school, a skydiving center, or an air taxi service (for example) may not pay as well or be as glamorous as working for the airlines or corporate aviation companies, but it might be a compromise you need to make in order to live happily.

Be sure to discuss all the benefits and also the downsides with your family. The more openly you discuss every aspect of the career, the easier it will be to avoid problems in your life later on.

Action Step 4: Schedule an Introductory Flight

Even if you are medically fit to fly, you can't be 100 percent sure that flying won't make you sick. What if you have a fear of heights that you aren't yet aware of? What if you have an inner ear problem that causes you to get dizzy in the air? What if flying simply is not what you expected it to be?

It's good to schedule an introductory flight before you start taking out loans or making down payments on a professional flight training course.

Go ahead and contact some of the nearest flight schools to schedule an introductory flight. Even better, if you have already researched where you want to do your flight training, you should try to do the introductory flight there.

When you schedule it, you should talk to them about your interest in becoming a pilot and ask if the flight can be treated as a normal flight lesson instead of just a sight-seeing flight.

For a smoother flight experience, it's good to do the introductory flight early in the morning or in the evening close to sunset (when the air is usually less bumpy).

Action Step 5: Choose a Flight School or an Airline Cadet Program

Choosing the right flight school is an important step in preparing for flight training. Remember to do your research, and go through all the factors described in the previous chapter.

If you want to work for a specific airline, then you should apply to its cadet program, if available. The application process may involve background screening and an interview process with pilot aptitude tests. You should prepare according to their instructions the best you can.

If you don't want to be tied to a single airline, you should narrow down your flight school options to two or three, and schedule times to visit them.

It's good to call the school beforehand and ask for a tour. If you simply walk in to a school, you may have to wait around until someone has time to talk to you. This is especially true if it's an aviation college that you're interested in.

After your visits, then it's time to choose the flight school that best fits your criteria.

Action Step 6: Choose a Flight Instructor

While you're visiting your chosen flight school, you should try to determine who your flight instructor will be. You can do this by talking to the flight school management during your visit, and asking them who you should expect to fly with given your planned starting date.

Whoever makes the school's student-instructor assignments should be able to check which instructors are available to accept new students at the time when you plan to start your training. You can ask to be introduced to your potential instructors, and try to schedule brief one-on-one meetings with them.

You're going to be spending countless hours in the air with this person, so there really is nothing more important than having a good instructor. And it's helpful if you and your instructor get along well. Even a brief meeting with different instructors can help you determine who might be the best instructor for you.

If the instructors are not available during your visit, you could also ask for their contact information and try to schedule informational interviews over coffee. You could also try to reach out to the instructors online if you can find their contact information through the flight school's website; not all instructors are listed on the websites, though.

Because of ever-changing flight schedules and student assignments, the school or the instructors may not be able to make any commitments at the time of your visit. You may have to delay this step until you actually start your flight training program. But if you're able to determine who you want to fly with, you can put in a request with the flight school early on.

Action Step 7: Get Financing

You obviously need to get financing before you can commit to flight training. After choosing your flight school, you should have a good estimate of your flight training expenses.

Now it's time to apply for loans, scholarships, grants, credit cards, or whatever other financing method you have decided to use. For a professional pilot training course, you may have to put down a deposit (but not the full price of the course) and provide proof that you can meet the financial requirements for the course.

This is especially true for international students training in the United States; you will normally need some degree of financial proof before you can even apply for a student visa.

Don't forget to get the list of different aviation scholarships you can download[1] with the other bonus materials here: https://funkypilot.com/bonus

Action Step 8: Get That Student Pilot Certificate

Before you start your flight training program, you should get that student pilot certificate I mentioned earlier. Your flight school will probably help you get one, but there's no need to wait. The earlier you get it, the faster you can progress to the solo flying stage.

You don't need it in order to take flight or ground lessons. But you will need to have it before your first solo flight. If you do accelerated flight training, you might be ready for your first solo within a week or two from your first flight lesson, so it's good to get this certificate as early as possible.

There is no fee for a student pilot certificate, and it has no expiration date. So there's no reason to wait until you actually start training to get it.

To be eligible for a student pilot certificate you need to be 16 years old, and be able to read, write and understand English. There are no other requirements set forth by the FAA. But remember, you need to be 17 years old before you can get your private pilot certificate.

You can apply for the student pilot certificate through the Integrated Airman Certification and Rating Application (IACRA).[2] https://iacra.faa.gov/IACRA/

Simply fill out all the required information in the online application (make sure to save it). Before submitting the application, you do need someone to verify your identity.

And that someone needs to be an FAA-certified flight instructor, a designated pilot examiner, or an employee at a Flight Standards district office. After verifying your identity, that person will help you submit the application.

It shouldn't be difficult to find a flight instructor who can help you with this. A good way to get it done is to fill out the application before your introductory flight.

After the flight, ask the instructor who flew with you to help you. There should not be any fee associated with this process. Once the application is submitted, your certificate will be mailed to you within about three weeks.

If you live near a Flight Standards district office (FSDO)[3] you could also fill out and print the FAA Form 8710-1[4] and take it to the FSDO yourself. They would in turn send it to the Airmen Certification Branch, which will mail you your student pilot certificate. But the easiest way is just to do it online through the IACRA website.

Although a student pilot certificate is required for solo flights, the certificate itself doesn't provide you with any privileges. You will still need a logbook endorsement from your instructor before you can do a solo flight. Your solo endorsement will specify the make and model of the aircraft you are allowed to fly, as well as some weather requirements.

Action Step 9: Get Some Study Materials

Professional flight training packages usually include a bunch of study materials. When I did my training, I was provided with a flight bag full of FAA handbooks, Jeppesen manuals, Gleim study guides, a FAR/AIM regulation book, and pilot operating handbooks for the different types of training airplanes I was going to fly.

Nowadays, you can get by without purchasing many physical books. In fact, you can get most of your books for free. On my resources page, I have links to over 30 different FAA handbooks and guides.

Those books contain all the knowledge required to complete your training. They may be a bit difficult to read, however, so you should expect to purchase a few training books during flight school. Not just yet, though.

For now, I would recommend you download at least the *Airplane Flying Handbook*, the *Pilot's Handbook of Aeronautical Knowledge*, and the *Aeronautical Information Manual*. And don't just download them—actually take the time to read and get familiar with them. Get the books from https://funkypilot.com/resources/.

You will be using them a lot during your training. They are fairly massive and overwhelming documents, so try not to be discouraged; they will be broken down in ground school and taught to you in a clear and concise manner.

Once you start your training, you'll have a better idea about whether you should purchase physical books. It can be much easier to study from physical books than from reading on a computer or tablet. But it's also a lot more expensive.

Action Step 10: Just Do It!

If you successfully completed all the previous steps, you can now fully commit to flight training and sign a flight-training contract.

You should have enough cash in the bank to pay for the training. You should have a happy spouse rooting for you at home. And you should have the best instructor in the world waiting for you at the flight school you chose!

So, go ahead and do it! Sign up for flight training and you will have an exciting future ahead of you!

Good luck!

FINAL WORDS

Did you enjoy this Book?

If this book somehow inspired you to pursue a career as a pilot, or if you otherwise enjoyed reading it, I would like to ask you a small favor; I would appreciate it very much if you could review the book on Amazon, Goodreads, or any other book review website that you prefer.

In Amazon or Goodreads, simply type in my name (Vesa Turpeinen), then choose this book to leave a review.

That would help other aspiring pilots, or readers who are interested in the subject, find the book. Even a sentence or two would be very helpful!

Join my Facebook Group!

Remember to also join me and other aspiring pilots in my Pilot Career Facebook Group (facebook.com/groups/pilotcareers/), where you can find more personalized advice based on your unique interests and circumstances.

Do you have Questions or Comments?

If you have any further questions or comments about the topics covered in this book, you can send me an email at vesa.turpeinen@funkypilot.com.

I wish you the best of luck with your new pilot career, should you choose to pursue it! Otherwise, best of luck with your chosen career—whatever it may be!

Happy Flying, Everyone!

...AND ONE MORE THING

The purpose of this book was to help you get started with flight training. Now, you probably still only have a vague idea about what to expect from the training process.

What do you do up in the air, anyway? How many exams do you need to take, and what do you need to do to study for them?

My second book—*Pilot Career Book 2*—will answer those questions for you. It covers the training process, from private pilot to commercial pilot, in detail. The book is available now, and you can get it from here: https://www.amazon.com/author/vesaturpeinen.

I also hope you sign up for my email list: https://funkypilot.com/bonus, so I can notify you when my other books are available!

www.funkypilot.com

A SPECIAL FREE GIFT FOR YOU!

As a THANK YOU for purchasing my book, I would like to give you FREE instant access to some bonus materials. The bonus materials include the following:

- List of Aviation Scholarships Applicable for Funding Your Flight Training
- Personality of a Pilot - Research Paper
- List of Questions to Ask When Choosing a Flight School
- Professional Pilot's Guide for Better Sleep and Jet Lag Recovery - 12 Proven Methods to Improve the Quality of Your Sleep

Get your bonus materials here:

https://funkypilot.com/bonus

FUNKYPILOT STORE DISCOUNT CODE

As I mentioned earlier, I started an online store (Funky-Pilot Store)[1] in late 2020. I didn't create it just to profit myself – instead, I want to help aspiring pilots finance their flight training through my business. 100% of my 2020 and 2021 profits will go to a flight training scholarship fund. At least 50% of 2022 will also go to the fund. After that, I will adjust the percentage, but it will never go below 25% — it's a permanent fund, and my goal is to donate more and more money into the fund every year.

I hope that doing something good for other people will help my business become profitable, and if it does, I hope other companies will follow the example. My dream is to grow the fund so much that there would be enough cash to fund full flight training for several students every year. The fund helps the students struggling for financing, and it also helps the flight schools and instructors who get to train the students.

Please, take a look at my website. You can help build the fund by purchasing anything from the store – no need to donate anything. To get 20% off from your first purchase, please use the code: PILOT2B during checkout!

**USE CODE AT CHECKOUT:
PILOT2B**

www.funkypilotstore.com

BECOME AN AFFILIATE!

If you want to earn some extra money for yourself, you can become a FunkyPilot Store affiliate. As an affiliate, you will earn a 5 to 10% commission on each sale you make by referring customers to our store. Your commission and benefits will increase the more you sell.

Our affiliate program is easy to join, sign up here https://funkypilotstore.goaffpro.com and start earning!

As an affiliate, you can share coupon codes with your friends on social media networks – they enjoy low prices while you get paid! And remember, most of our profits go towards flight training scholarships! For more information, contact affiliates@funkypilotstore.com

www.funkypilotstore.com

NOTES

About This Book

1. Example Endnote
2. Pilot Career Resources: https://www.funkypilot.com/resources

1. A Brief Story About My Life in Aviation

1. My personal blog: https://funkypilot.com/

3. Why Become a Pilot?

1. Boeing's 2020 Pilot Outlook: https://www.boeing.com/commercial/market/pilot-technician-outlook/
2. Pilot Career Facebook Group: http://facebook.com/groups/pilotcareers
3. United States Bureau of Labor Statistics pilot salary information: https://www.bls.gov/ooh/Transportation-and-Material-Moving/Airline-and-commercial-pilots.htm#tab-5
4. Corporate Pilot's Guide to Hotel Benefits blog post: https://funkypilot.com/2018/01/10/corporate-pilots-guide-to-hotel-benefits/
5. Catch me if You Can: https://www.imdb.com/title/tt0264464/?ref_=nv_sr_1

4. The Downsides of a Career in Aviation

1. Pilot Career Book 1 - Bonus Materials: https://funkypilot.com/bonus
2. Fundamentals of Aerospace Medicine - Cosmic Radiation NASA study: https://ntrs.nasa.gov/archive/nasa/casi.ntrs.nasa.gov/20070028831.pdf
3. 2013/59/EURATOM - Laying down basic safety standards for protection against the dangers arising from exposure to ionising radiation: https://ec.europa.eu/energy/sites/ener/files/documents/CELEX-32013L0059-EN-TXT.pdf

6. Is Flying for You?

1. Chuck Yeager: https://www.chuckyeager.com/
2. EasyJet Cadet Training: https://careers.easyjet.com/pilots/thinking-of-becoming-a-pilot/
3. SpiceJet Hiring Female Pilots: https://www.cnbctv18.com/aviation/spicejet-targets-33-female-pilots-in-its-crew-as-airlines-get-accused-of-paying-lip-service-to-diversity-3553341.htm
4. Jobs with Biggest Gender Pay Gap: https://www.nbcnews.com/know-your-value/feature/job-biggest-gender-pay-gap-ncna989521
5. Women in Aviation International: https://www.wai.org
6. Medical Conditions Considered Disqualifying by the FAA: https://www.faa.gov/licenses_certificates/medical_certification/faq/response6/
7. FAR 61.23 Medical Certificates - Requirements and Duration: https://www.ecfr.gov/cgi-bin/text-idx?SID=723e64f41f741acfa727a557ceb2d4fa&mc=true&node=pt14.2.61&rgn=div5#se14.2.61_123
8. FAA Aviation Medical Examiner locator: http://www.faa.gov/pilots/amelocator/

9. FAA MedXpress: https://medxpress.faa.gov/medxpress/
10. Free Colorblindness Test: https://colormax.org/color-blind-test/
11. Electronic Code of Federal Regulations Part 67: https://www.ecfr.gov/cgi-bin/text-idx?SID=d1of3a6eca97eff9c32de21f6b8a00ea&mc=true&node=pt14.2.67&rgn=div5
12. FAA Medical Certification website: https://www.faa.gov/pilots/medical/
13. Pilot Shortage in Japan: https://japantoday.com/category/national/pilots-retirement-age-to-be-raised-to-67-to-cope-with-shortage
14. AOPA Hazardous Attitudes Article: https://www.aopa.org/news-and-media/all-news/1999/september/flight-training-magazine/hazardous-attitudes
15. Jeppesen Aviation English: https://ww2.jeppesen.com/training-and-pilot-supplies/commercial-aviation-classroom-training/
16. Aviator College English Courses: https://www.aviator.edu/icao-aviation-english
17. EAA Free Introductory Flight: https://www.eaa.org/eaa/learn-to-fly/introductory-flights-for-free

8. The Cost of Training and How to Finance It

1. Florida Flyers Flight Academy: https://www.flightschoolusa.com/
2. Sunrise Aviation: https://flysunrise.com/
3. ATP Flight School: https://atpflightschool.com/airline-career-pilot-program/
4. SunState Aviation: https://www.sunstateaviation.com/aircraft-rental-and-rates/
5. American Airlines Cadet Program: http://www.aacadetacademy.com/CadetAcademy/program_costs/1

6. JetBlue Airways Cadet Program: https://pilots.jetblue.com/gateway-select

7. British Airways Cadet Program: https://careers.ba.com/future-pilots

8. L3 Airline Academy: https://www.l3commercialaviation.com/airline-academy/easa-pilot-training/easa-pilot-training-courses/british-airways-cadet-programme/

9. Pilot Career Centre — Cadet Programs: https://pilotcareercentre.com/Cadet-Programs

10. Eagle Jet FAA Pilot Program: http://www.eaglejet.net/AIRLINE-PILOT-PROGRAM.asp#Link1

11. Eagle Jet EASA Pilot Program: http://www.eaglejet.net/Airline-Pilot-Program.asp#Link3

12. Eagle Jet "Pay to Fly" Pricing: http://www.eaglejet.net/Pricing.asp

13. Aviator College Financial Aid: https://www.aviator.edu/title-iv-federal-financial-aid

14. Federal Student Aid Database: https://fafsa.ed.gov/spa/fsc/

15. Free Application for Federal Student Aid (FAFSA): https://studentaid.ed.gov/sa/fafsa

16. Federal Student Aid Loan Types: http://studentaid.ed.gov/sa/types/loans

17. U.S. Department of Education: http://www.ed.gov/

18. Embry-Riddle Aeronautical University financial aid: https://worldwide.erau.edu/admissions/financial-aid

19. University of North Dakota financial aid: https://und.edu/one-stop/financial-aid/

20. Spartan College of Aeronautics and Technology financial aid: https://www.spartan.edu/admissions/financial-aid/

21. Listing of Aviation Colleges: https://www.bestaviation.net/college

22. ATP Flight School financing: https://atpflightschool.com/financing/

23. Aircraft Owners and Pilots Association (AOPA) financing: https://www.aopa.org/news-and-media/all-news/2015/march/

03/aopa-offers-flight-training-financing
24. Pilot Finance Inc.: https://www.pilotfinance.com/
25. FunkyPilot Flight Training Scholarship: https://funkypilotstore.com/pages/about-us
26. U.S. Department of Veterans Affairs/GI Bill: https://www.benefits.va.gov/gibill/
27. American Airlines Cadet Program financing: http://www.aacadetacademy.com/CadetAcademy/program_costs/1
28. JetBlue Airways Cadet Program financing: https://pilots.jetblue.com/gateway-select

9. Choosing a Flight School

1. Pilot Career Centre - Cadet Programs: https://pilotcareercentre.com/Cadet-Programs
2. AOPA's Aviation Colleges page: https://www.aopa.org/training-and-safety/learn-to-fly/aviation-colleges
3. FunkyPilot Blog Aircraft Page: https://funkypilot.com/aviation/aircraft/
4. LinkedIn: https://www.linkedin.com

10. Time to Get Started!

1. Pilot Career Book 1 - Bonus Materials: https://funkypilot.com/bonus
2. Integrated Airman Certification and Rating Application (IACRA): https://iacra.faa.gov/IACRA/Default.aspx
3. Flight Standards district offices (FSDO): https://www.faa.gov/about/office_org/field_offices/fsdo/
4. FAA Form 8710-1: https://www.faa.gov/documentlibrary/media/form/faa_8710-1.pdf

FunkyPilot Store Discount Code

1. FunkyPilot Store: https://funkypilotstore.com

ABOUT THE AUTHOR

Vesa Turpeinen is a longtime aviator, pilot, and flight instructor. He is the former Chief Flight Instructor of the Chaoyang Flight College of CAUC and MBA graduate from Embry-Riddle Aeronautical University. Vesa grew up in Helsinki, Finland, and currently resides in Hangzhou, China.

This is Vesa's first of his two published books, and more of his aviation series will follow. Meanwhile, he welcomes everyone to read his stories in his aviation and travel blog: funkypilot.com.

Printed in Great Britain
by Amazon